D0888121

Old Roses
and
English Roses

DAVID AUSTIN

Foreword by Graham Stuart Thomas

Antique Collectors' Club

To my wife, Pat

Parts of this book first appeared in *The Heritage of the Rose* by David Austin, 1988, revised 1990

British Library Cataloguing in Publication Data: A catalogue record for this book is available from the British Library

Published for the Antique Collectors' Club by the Antique Collectors' Club Ltd.

Frontispiece: SHARIFA ASMA, an English Rose of great delicacy and charm

Printed in England by the Antique Collectors' Club Ltd., Woodbridge, Suffolk, on Consort Royal Supreme Matt from Donside Mills, Aberdeen, Scotland

Contents

Photographic Acknowledgements

David Knight, A.B.I.P.P., A.R.P.S., A.S.I.A. (Art and Design), of the School of Art and Design, The Polytechnic, Wolverhampton.

Michael Warren, A.B.I.P.P., A.M.P.A., who specialises in horticultural photography and has a large library of pictures.

Vincent Page, Picture Editor of *The Sunday Times Colour Supplement,* who possesses one of the largest collections of rose pictures, and who gave extensive and valuable assistance in the editing of photographs.

Claire Austin, B.A. (Hons.), who assists the author at his nursery, specialising in hardy plants.

Graham Stuart Thomas, O.B.E., V.M.H., D.H.M., V.M.M., formerly Garden Adviser to the National Trust and author of many books on gardening

Professor G. Fineschi, Italy, whose garden in Florence contains one of the finest collections of roses in Europe.

Other photographs are from R.C. Balfour, Harry Smith's Horticultural Photographic Collection, Paul Edwards, garden designer, and the following nurseries/nurserymen: Cants of Colchester, James Cocker & Sons, Dickson Nurseries Ltd., Fryer's Nurseries Ltd., R. Harkness & Co. Ltd., Le Grice Roses, John Mattock Ltd., Wisbech Plant Co. Ltd. and B.J. Tysterman.

Acknowledgements

I wish to express my thanks to a number of people who have helped me in the production of this book.

Graham Stuart Thomas for reading the manuscript and making numerous helpful suggestions.

Barry Ambrose of the Royal Horticultural Society, Wisley, for much help, encouragement and practical advice, including suggestions for plants for association with roses.

My publisher, Diana Steel, of the Antique Collectors' Club, who has allowed me an unusual amount of latitude and been very understanding throughout the production of this book, and Cherry Lewis, her assiduous and sympathetic Editor.

Diane Ratcliff and Doreen Pike for typing the scripts and much other help.

Foreword

Graham Stuart Thomas, O.B.E., V.M.H., D.H.M., V.M.M.

My memories of David Austin go back to the early 1950s when he used to make an annual visit to my first commercial collection of Old French Roses. He was, like me, almost bowled over by their unique beauty and gradually built up a selection from them. I think it was during our visit to the Paris rose gardens with Gordon Rowley that he first stated that one of his main aims in life was to breed roses of a shrubby nature. He had already made a start. We could all see that British, French and American breeders were intent on creating more and more hybrids set in the moulds of the Hybrid Teas and Floribundas, oblivious of the fact that only slight progress — of ever larger flowers and brighter colours — was likely to occur. They all had it firmly fixed in their minds that lovers of the rose simply desired bush roses along these stereotyped lines. (In this they were, and ever have been, encouraged by the competitive trials of the leading rose societies.) They had forgotten that the rose was originally a shrub. The Reverend Joseph Pemberton was of the same mind about the matter earlier in this century when he was producing 'Penelope', 'Felicia', 'Cornelia' and others of the Hybrid Musks. These did not become popular at the time because nobody was then looking for shrub roses, apart from the species which had always been favoured by shrub specialists.

It is now part of rose history that the resurgence in popularity of the Old Roses since the mid-1950s has resulted in dedicated groups of their admirers being formed throughout the English-speaking world, though it is improbable that anyone will try seriously to raise fresh varieties along the old lines; the old varieties reached a perfection of their own and are not likely to be surpassed. Having once broken into the storehouse of beauty exhibited by the shrub roses, I am sure there is no stopping the movement. The bush Hybrid Teas and Floribundas have earned their special popularity through providing floral colour from midsummer until autumn, but during the rest of the year they are not particularly attractive. It was obvious what was needed: shrubs of grace and beauty in a variety of sizes, with good foliage, capable of producing

8

flowers of all shapes — doubles and singles, simple or sophisticated — in a range of colours and fragrances, so that they could play their part in the general furnishing of the garden, and not merely in beds on lawn or paving. It was such thoughts as these which spurred David on to use some of his spare time as a farmer to raise his first seedlings.

I think it would be right to say that David is a nonconformist when it comes to roses. After all, why should a new rose have to conform to the stereotyped lines of modern bush roses, so freely used for bedding? When I asked one of the panel of judges of the Royal National Rose Society why so few of David's roses had received any recognition I was told they were 'too lanky'. I realised afterwards that this meant they did not conform to the standards laid down for modern bedding roses nor to the Society's version of a shrub rose, which is really nothing more than an overgrown Floribunda. We need graceful shrub roses for gardens of all sizes. But just think how these judging criteria limit our appreciation of a great shrub rose. Should it be said that the splendid 'Nevada' or 'Frühlingsgold', 'Fritz Nobis' or 'Golden Wings' are too lanky? We should welcome more roses of such superlative value, but there is also a great need for shrub roses of similar grace, beauty, individual charm and scent for smaller gardens; roses of, say, three to five feet in height and width, which will bloom from summer until autumn. This is what David has set himself to produce.

Breeding from garden roses is very unpredictable. The plants are of such mixed origin, with so many generations behind them, that to cross a pink rose with a white, for instance, may result in a whole range of colours including red, purple and yellow. We must remember when contemplating the welter of dazzling colours of modern roses, that these vivid tones all stem from hybridizing the Old Roses with three species only from among the 150 existing around the Northern Hemisphere. First the pale yellow of *Rosa gigantea* and the crimson of *R. chinensis,* followed by the strong yellows and flames of *R. foetida.* Crosses with these three put into reverse the continuation of the whites, soft pinks, mauves, purples and maroons of the Old French Roses. As if these giant strides were not enough for over a hundred years of breeding, a strident new colour — pelargonidin, a vermilion of neon-brilliance — suddenly cropped up without initiation by man sometime shortly after 1929.

It has been my privilege for some years to visit David's rose fields and see the results of his labours. Though his stud book records the many thousands of crosses made each year, owing to the unpredictability of breeding in a non-stereotyped group of plants it seems to me that almost anything may happen, but to his experienced eye the results are more recognisable. The result is that from the initial sowing of the precious grains (any one of which may just as well develop into a plant of superlative beauty as into one which may prove to be an utter dud) selection must be made from the first flowering onwards. This happens in the first year with repeat-flowering roses. Any likely candidates are propagated and after three or four years and several acres of plants, perhaps ten of a kind may be the reward. Further assessment of the growth, foliage, flower and scent will be made two or three times a week, at different times of the day, for three or four months. And in the meantime successive years' crosses will be made and sown, all to be watched likewise. Assessing and reassessing each variety is difficult. Wandering down the rows of a morning may bring quite different opinions from following the same paths later in the day. It is only by ruthless selection and the destruction of over ninety per cent that a handful of good plants may be re-propagated, perhaps a hundred of each. If these in bulk pass muster after three or more years, a few of them may be named and may prove a success, such as 'Mary Rose' and my own namesake. It is interesting to recall that the latter was the only rich soft yellow amongst hundreds of seedlings. But on looking back one can see that it has ever been a rare colour, cropping up first in the old Noisettes, such as 'Alister Stella Gray', and then again in 'Lady Hillingdon' and the Hybrid Musk 'Buff Beauty', with pale echoes in 'Barbara Richards' and 'Golden Dawn'.

We are very fortunate that David has had the initiative and vision, persistence and faith, to have given us the selection — from his thousands of crosses — which are named and described in Chapter 4 under his chosen title of English Roses. It is high time that his roses should receive proper evaluation, and who better than by the raiser, who, as he rightly claims, should know more than any one else about the failings of each seedling as well as its assets.

There is no doubt that David is well on the way to giving us a new class, the small graceful shrub of repeat-flowering habit which will fit into our complex gardens of today. He has fortunately been able to bring to his work the eye not only of a commercial nurseryman but also that of a lover of gardens and the imagination that goes with both.

It must be encouraging to him to know that his productions are already being listed by rose nurseries in ten different countries.

I am sure that the opinions expressed in this book will help us all to reassess the manifold beauties of Old Roses and English Roses.

COTTAGE ROSE, *few English Roses flower with such regularity as this. Dainty, medium sized flowers throughout the summer.*

Introduction

Garden roses fall into two very different groups which are usually described as the Old Roses and the Modern Roses. Most of the Old Roses were introduced before 1900, while most of the Modern Roses were introduced after that date. There is, however, a great deal of overlap on both sides of that date. The Old Roses have flowers of quite a different style to those of the Modern. The beauty of the Old Rose lies in the open flower and a more natural shrubby habit of growth, while the Modern Roses (by which I mean the Hybrid Teas and Floribundas of our gardens today) are bedding roses of short, upright habit whose beauty usually lies in the unfolding bud.

The Old Garden Roses have been with us for centuries, starting almost at the dawn of civilisation in the Middle East – spreading first to Greece and later to Rome and thence to Europe as a whole. They are distinguished by their open flowers, usually in the form of a rosette, but are often of cupped shape and sometimes of a more domed shape with recurving petals. Such flowers may have many petals or few; they may be loosely built or closely packed with petals, resulting in a great variety of shapes. They may also be double or semi-double. Above all, the majority of them are very fragrant. Their great disadvantages are that they flower but once in a summer and have limited colour range.

The Old Roses began to lose their popularity in the latter part of the 19th century, and by the early part of the 20th century had almost disappeared from our gardens in the face of competition from the all-conquering Hybrid Teas. Fortunately for us, no sooner had they almost disappeared, when certain collectors started to preserve them in their gardens. It is interesting to note that George Paul, writing in the Royal Horticultural Society's Journal in 1896, said: 'Wanted: a refuge for the old roses where they may be found again when tastes change.' He was, in fact, showing remarkable insight, for within little more than a quarter of a century such outstanding gardeners as Edward Bunyard, G.N. Smith, George Beckwith, Maud Messel, Constance Spry, Ruby Fleischmann, Murray Hornibrook, A.T.Johnson, Bobbie James, Anastasia Law, Vita Sackville-West and others, were already gathering together collections of Old Roses.

It is, however, to Graham Thomas that we owe the greatest debt. It was he who put together all these collections into one great collection – and indeed added many more, as Nursery Manager first at Hillings & Co. of Woking and later at Sunningdale Nurseries. His collection of different varieties numbered well into four figures, and from these nurseries the old varieties spread into many gardens in the United Kingdom and eventually into nurseries around the world, so that we now have a movement which is continually gathering momentum.

Graham Thomas did more than just preserve these roses – he changed the way we looked at them through his three volumes entitled *The Old Shrub Roses, Shrub Roses of Today* and *Climbing Roses Old and New.* In these books he observes the Rose so acutely and describes roses so well, that it would be difficult to improve on him. Indeed, almost all subsequent writers on this subject have felt the need to state their debt to him, and for me perhaps more so than for others, as he has been my friend and adviser over the last thirty-five years.

More recently, others have taken up this work, such as Nancy Steen in New Zealand, Pat Wiley of Roses of Yesterday and Today in California, Peter Beales, who has gathered together one of the largest commercial collections of roses, Trevor Griffiths in New Zealand, who has another exceptionally large commercial collection, and many others too numerous to name or unknown to me.

At our Nurseries in Albrighton we have bred a range of roses which we have called English Roses. These are the result of crossing Old Roses with Modern Roses. In the English Roses we have combined the open or rosette type flower of the Old Roses, with the repeat-flowering chracteristics of the Modern Roses. English Roses are in fact in the nature of repeat-flowering Old Roses. They also retain the rich fragrance of Old Roses and have a wide range of colouring.

In this book I cover all the most worthwhile of the Old Roses and carry this on to their natural successors, the English Roses. The two go together to form a natural group and are an ideal subject for a book. I have for convenience also included the Rugosa Roses, which bear some affinity to the Old Roses.

A second volume will cover the remainder of the garden roses – that is to say Modern Shrub Roses, the Hybrid Teas and Floribundas, the numerous and very beautiful Climbers and Ramblers and the Wild Species Roses. It will also include a chapter on the use of all kinds of roses in the garden.

MARIE LOUISE, *Damask Rose. One of the most sumptuous of the Old Roses.*

CHAPTER 1
The Rose

Throughout the history of western civilisation, from the earliest times to the present day, the rose has been the flower closest to the heart of man. In Greek mythology Aphrodite, goddess of love, was regarded as the creator of the rose, which was supposed to have arisen from a mixture of her tears and the blood of her wounded lover Adonis. In Roman legend it was said to have sprung from the blood of Venus. Again and again we find it appearing in ancient history as a symbol of love and beauty, and sometimes of licentiousness and excess.

With the rise of Christianity the rose was at first looked upon with disapproval due to its pagan past, but this attitude soon changed, and we find the rose becoming intertwined with the Christian faith: for example, the rosary and the idea of the five petals of the rose representing the five wounds of Christ. Indeed, it was the church which was in a large degree responsible for carrying the rose across Europe to many lands.

Although we in the West, and in Britain in particular, like to think of the rose as being very much our own, this is in fact by no means entirely true. Roses appear at one time or another in association with Brahma, Buddha, Mahomet, Vishnu and Confucius, and the origins of the roses we enjoy today lie in a large degree in the lands of the Middle and Far East.

The earliest known representation of a rose was found in Crete, dated somewhere between 1700 and 2000 B.C. Since that time it has appeared in painting and sculpture, on pottery and fabrics, and as a decoration of all kinds, in all ages and in many lands.

If we consider the rose as decoration, it soon becomes clear that it stands supreme above all other flowers. Indeed it is difficult to walk into any house in the West without finding some representation of a rose. This, I think, illustrates better than anything else the very special place the rose holds in our lives. When I was talking to the chief designer from one of our largest firms of pottery manufacturers, he told me that the rose is by far the most popular decoration for china and pottery, the demand for rose designs exceeding those of all other flower designs put together.

The history of the rose has been written and rewritten on numerous occasions and makes intriguing reading. I do not intend to go over this ground again, except in so far as it helps us to understand and appreciate our subject. Nor is it necessary to go too deeply into the long history of roses to realise how important they have always been. Since those far-off days when we first hear of the rose many flowers have come to the fore as garden plants, but none has come anywhere near to supplanting it.

Today roses are to be found in almost every garden in the country in which there are any flowers at all. They are also to be found in almost every country in the world, sometimes struggling in the most unsuitable of climates. What is the fascination of this flower? How is it that the rose has always been the best loved of all flowers? It seems to have the ability to evoke by its beauty (and, to some degree, through the long accumulation of its history) many of the emotions, principles, desires and joys fundamental to the spirit of man, and to do this as no other flower can. For this reason, it is worthy of closer attention than we would afford other flowers; for the rose is more than other flowers — it is part of the very fabric of our lives; it has about it a humanity that we do not find in any other flower. It is only necessary to consider the few brief notes I have made so far to realise how true this is.

In the flower of a rose there are many flowers. It is seldom quite the same on any two days. From the opening bud to the fall of the flower, at every turn of its petals as they unfold, it is always presenting us with a different picture. Its colouring, too, is the same: perhaps deep and rich at the centre, maybe softer towards the outer edges, but the balance will always be changing, sometimes paling with time, or taking on a new hue, or occasionally intensifying. The flower varies according to where it is grown, from garden to garden, from one soil to another. It varies according to weather conditions; it will be quite different on a sunny day than on one which is cool and overhung. It will take on one appearance in early summer and quite another in the autumn. Here perhaps is one reason why we do not easily tire of it.

Between one variety and another, from one class to another, and from species to species, the rose has many forms. The flower may, for example, be in the form of a rosette as in the old Alba Rose 'Queen of Denmark'; it may be a rounded cup as in the Bourbon Rose 'Reine Victoria'. There are the heavy voluptuous blooms of *Rosa centifolia,* the wide open semi-double flowers of the Damask 'Celsiana' with its long stamens.

Then there is fragrance, which has been described as the very soul of a rose, and here we find no less diversity. The sense of smell is a hard one to tie down; it is the least developed of all our senses, yet it has great power to move us. Various people at various times have found the scent of many different flowers in roses and I doubt if there is a wider range to be found in any other flower. Not only are there the rich, heady fragrances of the Old Roses, as in the Centifolias and Damasks, which have been handed down over the ages to many roses of the present day, but there is also the myrrh-like fragrance of many of the English Roses. And more than these too, for the scent of violet, clove, peony, lilac, apple, raspberry and others have been detected in various roses. The great majority of roses are fragrant, usually strongly so, but in some it is a slight fragrance, in a few it is barely detectable, but it is almost never entirely absent.

Man has taken a wild flower and over many centuries, at first by the selection of chance seedlings and later by design, moulded it to his wishes. The rose is a flower that belongs in the main to those parts of the garden that are close to the house, and those parts most closely controlled by the gardener. Here it is always with us as we pass; one of those small but not insignificant parts of our life that makes it worth the living.

With all this, the rose is the most practical of plants, often flowering intermittently from early summer to the coming of the first frosts. Once planted it will live for many years, and while it will certainly reward careful cultivation, many of its varieties will survive quite happily with little or no attention. Even those with no particular feeling for flowers can plant it in the knowledge that it is not going to give very much trouble. It is a flower for all people, from the great garden to the smallest suburban plot. What other flower can combine so many qualities? It is small wonder that the rose is known as the 'Queen of Flowers'.

Old Roses and English Roses are but a part of the great family of the rose, but an increasingly important part for the majority of discerning gardeners. These are the subject of this book.

A BORDER *at David Austin's gardens, illustrating the natural growth of Old Roses.* *'Ispahan', Damask Rose; 'Nozomi'; 'F.J. Grootendorst', Rugosa Rose; 'Cardinal de Richelieu', Gallica Rose.*

CHAPTER 2

Old Roses I

In this chapter I include all those classes which were established prior to the introduction of the repeat-flowering China Rose at the end of the 18th century, and which had such a revolutionary effect on the development of the rose and eventually led to the Hybrid Teas and Floribundas of the present day. That is to say the Gallicas, the Damasks, the Albas, the Centifolias and the Moss Roses. As most readers will be aware these are not small upright bushes, as are Modern Hybrid Teas, but genuine shrubs like any other shrub in the garden. Their growth will reach somewhere in the region of 4 to 6ft. according to variety, although there are among them many smaller shrubs that fit nicely into a small garden.

The formation of their flowers is quite different to that which we have become accustomed to today. In the Modern Rose the ideal lies in the bud with its high-pointed centre, and this is indeed often beautiful, but the disadvantage is that the mature flower tends to be muddled and almost completely lacking in form. Old Roses are quite different; their buds, though often charming, are likely to open as small cups, with little petals developing within, but it is as the flower gradually expands into the full bloom that its true beauty is revealed. At this later stage it can take on many forms: it may remain cupped, it may become flat with many petals, or it may reflex at the edges to form an almost domed flower. Between these shapes there are many gradations. The flower may also, of course, be semi-double, exposing an airy bunch of stamens at the centre. Thus we have a bloom that is beautiful at all stages, from the opening of the bud to the eventual fall of the petals. It is this variety of form that makes these roses so worth while. Fine as the Hybrid Tea may be, the Old Roses offer so much more scope, and for this reason we have, at our nursery, thought it worth while to proceed further with the breeding of roses of the old type. I shall be discussing these in Chapters 4 and 5.

It has to be admitted that Old Roses are rather limited in their colour range. We have white through pink all the way to a maroon-crimson, mauve and purple — all colours often of exceptional purity and softness of tone. Susan Williams-Ellis (who has spent many weeks at our nursery painting roses for her Portmeirion Pottery) speaking in terms of fabrics has suggested that these are like vegetable dyes in comparison with the harsher 'chemical' colours of Modern Roses. I think this puts it rather well. There are, unfortunately, only one or two yellows and not many whites, although 'Madame Hardy' and 'Madame Legras de St. Germain' can produce some of the most perfect blooms. Pink is the true colour of the rose, and in the Old Roses it often has a clarity seldom found elsewhere. The colour crimson is seldom pure in these early roses, but it does have the great virtue of turning to wonderful shades of purple, violet and mauve.

The Old Roses of this section do have one disadvantage, if in fact it can be truly described as a disadvantage; they flower only once in a season, whereas their successors are repeat flowering. It should, however, be borne in mind that we expect no more of any other shrub. We do not, for example, expect repeat flowering of the lilac or the rhododendron. If your garden is reasonably large, you may not wish to have all your roses in flower throughout the summer, even though you will probably like to have at least some in bloom later in the season. You may prefer that they should take their place in due season, like any other flower. It should also be remembered that a rose which flowers but once tends to give a better show for that limited period, during which it is able to devote all its energy to one glorious burst of flowers. It will also usually form a more shapely shrub for, unlike bush roses, shrub roses produce long growth from the base of the plant. This does not flower in the first season but subsequently sends out flowering branches. It is this strong growth that forms the basic structure of a well-shaped shrub which is not only more pleasing to the eye, but which also displays its flowers in a more natural and satisfactory manner. In addition to this the plant is likely to be much more robust because it has not had to expend its energy on the continual production of flowers.

Almost all these roses are over one hundred years old, and a few may well be over a thousand years old. There must have been many more of their brethren who have fallen by the wayside. Those that remain really are great survivors. It is, therefore, not surprising that they are extremely tough and hardy. It is our experience that they are also more disease resistant than most roses, mildew being their worst fault, though this is not difficult to control. They are easy to grow and will do well with minimal care, although a little extra attention can yield rich rewards.

The rose has received far more attention from the plant breeder than any other flower, so it may seem strange so many gardeners should turn back to the beginning and start growing varieties from the distant past. There is little doubt this has something to do with the attractions of the antique, and I see no reason to decry this. There is, however, much more to the Old Roses than this, for they possess a very special charm that is not always to be found in roses of more recent date.

It is my personal opinion that we are today much too obsessed with the past, and often too little concerned with the creations of our own time. If we consider the devotion that we put into the preservation of old buildings and how little concern we show for new ones, it sometimes seems a little unhealthy. Having said this, there is a certain satisfaction to be gained from the sheer permanence of these roses; we have had time to get to know them and to love them, something that cannot be said for Modern Roses that come and go with bewildering speed. In spite of this, it cannot be stressed too strongly that these are not mere curiosities but first-class shrubs in their own right, and their gentle colours and more natural growth melt perfectly into the garden scheme. Finally, but by no means least, it is hardly necessary to say that their fragrance excels that of the majority of those which have come after them. Considered as a group they are, to me, still the most beautiful of all roses.

The naming of Old Roses is always a source of controversy and many Old Rose enthusiasts like to show their knowledge on the subject. These roses suffered a long period of neglect before re-emerging in our time, and inevitably many names were lost. Although a great deal of research has gone into finding the correct names this has not always been possible. A description found in an old book or catalogue may have been adequate for the gardeners of that time, but it is frequently insufficient for us to give a name to a particular rose. It has often been necessary simply to do the best that we can, and, in fact, this does not matter very much, for as we all know, a rose by any other name will smell as sweet. The important thing is to agree on a name so that we all know what we are talking about.

Gallica Roses

Rosa gallica is a native of central and southern Europe. It forms an upright shrub of 3ft. in height which suckers freely, with slender stems and many small thorns. It bears deep pink flowers of 2 to 3ins. across, followed by round, red hips. Our garden Gallicas have been developed over the centuries from this species.

Although so much of the history of Old Roses is shrouded in mystery it is safe to assume that the Gallicas are the oldest of garden roses and have been involved, to a greater or lesser extent, in the development of all the four other classes of Old Roses. Their influence is present, at least in some small degree, in nearly all our garden roses down to the present. Long before they received their name, their predecessors were grown by both the Greeks and Romans and almost certainly by others before them. Although they are the oldest of the truly Old Roses they also became the most highly developed. In 1629 the great English botanist and gardener John Parkinson listed twelve varieties. A little later the Dutch began raising seedlings to produce new varieties. It was not long before this activity spread to France, where breeding was carried out on a large scale and they became known as Gallicas. Soon after 1800 there were said to be over one thousand varieties. Most of these have long since been lost, but we still have more of them than any other group of the truly 'old' roses, and these still include some of the most beautiful roses that can be grown today.

Not surprisingly, all this work led to highly developed flowers in a variety of colours. These tend to be in the stronger shades: deep pinks and near crimsons, as well as rich mixtures of purple, violet and mauve.

BELLE DE CRÉCY, *one of the most attractive of the Gallica Roses.*

CARDINAL DE RICHELIEU, *one of the darkest of all Gallica Roses.*

There are a number of good striped varieties as well as others that are attractively mottled, marbled or flecked, and there are also a few soft pinks, though these are probably hybrids of other classes. No other Old Rose produces such subtle and fascinating mixtures of colour. They are nearly all very fragrant.

The Gallica Rose or, as it is sometimes called, the 'Rose of Provins', is not difficult to recognise. It usually forms a small shrub, generally not more than 4ft. in height, with strong rather upright growth and numerous small, bristly thorns. The leaves are oval, pointed at the tip, of rather rough texture and often dark green in colour. The flowers are usually held either singly or in threes, and the buds are typically of spherical shape.

These roses are excellent garden subjects, with low, easily managed growth that is ideal for the smaller garden. They will, if required, grow in poor, even gravelly soil, and demand a minimum of attention. If grown on their own roots they will sucker freely and quickly spread across a border. Although they are often effective when grown in this manner they can become a problem, and for this reason it is usually better to plant budded stock and not to plant too deeply.

ALAIN BLANCHARD. This variety has almost single flowers of deep purple-crimson, with contrasting golden stamens, the colour later turning to a purple which is attractively dotted and mottled with pink. Its growth is thorny, about 4ft. in height, with pale green foliage. Fragrant. Probably a Gallica/Centifolia cross. Bred by Vibert (France), introduced 1839.

ANAÏS SÉGALAS. This rose has perfectly shaped flowers which open flat and are well filled with petals, showing a green eye at the centre. The colour is a rich mauve-crimson, turning with age to a pale lilac-pink. It forms a low-growing, branching and free-flowering bush with light green foliage. Strong fragrance. Height 3ft. Vibert (France), introduced 1837.

ASSEMBLAGE DES BEAUTÉS ('Rouge Eblouissante'). Very double flowers of a vivid cherry-red, unusual amongst Gallicas; later becoming tinged with mauve, the petals reflexing almost to a ball, with a button eye at the centre. Very fragrant. Height 4ft. Introduced 1823.

BELLE DE CRÉCY. One of the finest, most free-flowering and reliable of Gallica Roses. On opening the flowers are a cerise-pink mixed with mauve, later turning to soft parma-violet and ultimately to lavender-grey; a wonderful succession of tints. They are shapely in form, the petals opening wide and reflexing to expose a button centre. A very rich fragrance. This variety will grow to about 4ft. in height and about 3ft. across. Bred prior to 1848. See page 22.

BELLE ISIS. A charming little rose of short growth that is ideal for the small garden. The flowers are not large but are full petalled, opening flat, neatly formed and of a delicate flesh-pink colour. It has tough, sturdy growth, with many prickles and small light green leaves. Its origins are something of a mystery as it is unusual to find so delicate a pink among the Gallicas, but it is probable that one of its parents was a Centifolia. It has the unusual fragrance of myrrh, and this would seem to indicate there is also Ayrshire 'Splendens' in its make up, for this scent was unique to those roses. Height 3ft. Bred by Parmentier (Belgium), introduced 1845.

BURGUNDY ROSE ('Parviflora', 'Pompon de Burgogne'). A charming miniature Gallica which forms a dense, very short jointed shrub, with very small dark green pointed leaves and tiny claret-coloured pompon flowers made up of numerous small petals. It is as though a large shrub had shrunk in all its parts, resulting in something quite unlike any other rose. The growth is about 3ft. in height. It can become rather too narrowly upright, but careful clipping will enable it to maintain its shape. In existence before 1664.

CAMAIEUX. One of the most pleasing of the striped roses. Its flowers are only loosely double but of shapely formation. They are white and heavily striped and splashed with a crimson that soon turns to purple, later becoming pale lilac and remaining attractive at all stages. There is a sweet and spicy fragrance. It forms a small shrub of about 3ft. in height. Introduced 1830.

CARDINAL DE RICHELIEU. One of the darkest of all roses. The flowers are mauvish-pink in the bud, becoming mauve, and ending in the richest pure purple. They are quite small and as they develop the petals reflex back almost forming a ball. This is an excellent garden shrub, developing into an arching mound of growth with dark green leaves and few thorns. It requires good cultivation and fairly severe pruning if it is to attain its full potential, otherwise the flowers may be rather insignificant. It is advisable to thin out the shrub by the annual removal of some of its older growth. The height is 5ft. by 4ft. across. Fragrant. It is said to have been bred by Laffay of France in 1840, but may have been bred in Holland by Van Sian and originally named 'Rose Van Sian'. See page 23.

CHARLES DE MILLS. The largest flowered and most spectacular of the Old Roses. Each bloom has numerous evenly-placed petals which open so flat that they give the impression of having been sliced off with a sharp knife. The colour is rich purple-crimson gradually turning to pure purple. It is an erect grower but forms a rather floppy shrub of 4ft. in height and may require some support. Unfortunately there is no more than a slight fragrance. Breeder and date of introduction not known.

CRAMOISI PICOTÉ. A pretty and unusual little rose with small, full, almost pompon flowers which are crimson in the bud, opening to a deep pink with crimson at the edges. The growth is short and compact with small dark green leaves. Little fragrance. Height 3ft. Bred by Vibert (France), introduced 1834.

CHARLES DE MILLS, *the largest of the Gallica Roses.*

DUC DE GUICHE, *a Gallica Rose with magnificent heavy blooms.*

DUCHESSE D'ANGOULÊME', *a Gallica Rose of unusually delicate colouring.*

D'AGUESSEAU. This rose has the brightest red colouring to be found among the Gallicas. For this reason we find it is in great demand — perhaps greater demand than its qualities warrant. Its colour is a bright cerise-scarlet although this soon fades to cerise-pink. The flowers are full petalled and fragrant, the growth strong with ample foliage. Height 5ft. Bred by Vibert (France), introduced 1837.

DUC DE GUICHE. A magnificent Gallica with large flowers of a rich wine-crimson shaded with purple. They have many petals and are beautifully formed, opening at first to a cup and gradually reflexing. It is one of the finest of its class, but in a dry season the colour can become dull and altogether less pleasing, particularly in light soils. Height about 4ft. Fragrant. Bred by Prévost, introduced 1829. See page 27.

DUCHESSE D'ANGOULÊME. This little charmer is probably not wholly Gallica. The delicacy of its transparent blush-pink globular flowers, which hang so gracefully from its arching growth, strongly suggests some other influence — *Rosa centifolia* has been suggested, but it is difficult to be sure. It has few thorns, light green foliage and a spreading growth to about 3ft. in height and as much across. It was, at one time, also known as the 'Wax Rose'. Bred by Vibert (France), prior to 1827. See page 27.

DUCHESSE DE BUCCLEUGH. A variety with unusually large flowers that open flat and quartered with a button eye. Their colour is an intense magenta-pink which does not appeal to everyone. The growth is very strong and upright, to 6ft. in height, with fine luxurious foliage. One of the latest of the Gallicas to flower. Bred by Robert (France), introduced 1846.

DUCHESSE DE MONTEBELLO. A rather loose-growing shrub bearing sprays of soft pink full-petalled flowers of open-cupped formation. These have a delicate charm and blend nicely with its grey-green foliage. It is unlikely that it is a true Gallica. I have used it for breeding purposes crossing it with repeat-flowering English Roses and, much to my surprise, obtained a proportion of repeat-flowering seedlings. This would suggest that it was itself the result of a cross with a repeat-flowering rose. Such mysteries contribute much to the interest of Old Roses. A beautiful rose with a sweet fragrance. Height 4ft. Bred by Laffay (France), introduced prior to 1829. See page 31.

DU MAÎTRE D'ÉCOLE. A variety producing some of the largest flowers found among Gallicas. They are full petalled and open flat and quartered, later reflexing to reveal a button centre. Their colour is a

EMPRESS JOSEPHINE, *Gallica Rose. An excellent Old Rose.*

deep pink, gradually turning to lilac-pink and taking on mauve and coppery shading as the flowers age. The growth is lax, about 3 or 4ft. in height, arching under the weight of its heavy, fragrant blooms. Meillez (France), 1840.

EMPRESS JOSEPHINE. The origins of this rose are not known. If it did exist in the time of Empress Josephine, it certainly did not bear her name, which it acquired quite recently. It is, however, an entirely appropriate name, as it is one of the most beautiful Old Roses and Josephine perhaps did more than anyone else to establish and encourage interest in roses throughout Europe, gathering together at Malmaison the largest collection of roses ever established up to her time. This variety is far removed from the typical Gallica and is classed as *Rosa x francofurtana.* It is probably a hybrid of *R. cinnamomea.* The flowers are semi-double with wavy petals of an unusual papery appearance. Their colour is a rich tyrian rose veined with a deeper shade. Unlike the majority of Old Roses, the flowers are followed by a fine crop of large turbinate hips. 'Empress Josephine' forms a low, shapely, rather flat growing bush some 3ft. in height, with very coarse textured grey-green foliage and few thorns. Excellent in every way, the only possible complaint being that it has no more than a faint fragrance. It has one close relative, 'Agatha', which is of the same class, but which is an altogether taller and coarser rose with, rather surprisingly, an intense fragrance.

GEORGES VIBERT. Rather small flowers which open flat, with narrow quilled petals of blush pink striped with light crimson. The growth is narrow and upright, about 5ft. in height, with many thorns and unusually small leaves. Bred by Robert (France), 1853.

GLOIRE DE FRANCE. A small shrub with somewhat spreading growth of 3ft. in height and rather more across. It bears beautifully shaped full lilac-pink flowers with reflexing petals which hold their colour at the centre while paling with age towards the edges. Bred prior to 1819.

HYPPOLYTE. A tall, vigorous shrub of 5ft. in height, with few thorns and small dark green leaves. The flowers, too, are small, flat at first, later reflexing into a ball-like formation. The colour is mauve-violet.

NESTOR. Lilac-pink flowers, deepening towards the centre, opening cupped, later becoming flat and quartered and gradually taking on mauve and grey tints. It has almost thornless growth of 4ft. in height. Introduced about 1846.

DUCHESSE DE MONTEBELLO, *an unusual blush-pink Gallica Rose.*

SURPASSE TOUT, *a typical, strongly coloured Gallica Rose.*

31

OFFICINALIS (the 'Apothecaries' Rose'). This historic rose is said to be the 'Red Rose of Lancaster', the emblem chosen by the House of Lancaster at the time of the Wars of the Roses, and there is little doubt it is the oldest cultivated form of the Gallica Rose that we have. It seems to have first appeared in Europe in the town of Provins, south east of Paris, where it was used in the making of perfume. It was said to have been brought there by Thibault Le Chansonnier on his return from the Crusades. Thibault IV, King of Navarre, wrote the poem *Le Roman de la Rose* in about 1260, and in it he refers to this rose as the rose from the 'Land of the Saracens'. Whatever the truth may be, this is a rose of great antiquity. For centuries it was grown for its medicinal qualities, and for this reason it is known as the 'Apothecaries' Rose'. Today we appreciate it for its excellent garden qualities, for it certainly deserves a place among the very finest of garden shrubs of any kind. It forms low branching growth, carries its semi-double light crimson fragrant flowers (with golden stamens) nicely poised above ample dark green foliage, blooms very freely, and provides a most satisfactory effect

ROSA MUNDI, *a Gallica Rose providing a wonderful massed effect.*

in the border. If grown on its own roots it will quickly spread by suckering and might well be used on banks and in other areas where ground cover is required. Budded on a stock it will grow to about 4ft. in height and about the same across. The colour varies widely according to climate and season and is much paler under hot conditions. In autumn it produces small round hips which are not without ornamental value.

POMPON PANACHÉE. A pretty little miniature-flowered rose with neatly-formed blooms that have deep pink stripes on a cream ground. They are held in ones and twos on wiry upright stems with small leaves. Erect growth of 3 or 4ft. in height.

PRÉSIDENT DE SÉZE ('Jenny Duval'). A perfect bloom of this rose can be more beautiful than any other to be found among the Gallicas. Its attractive lilac buds open to magnificent large full-petalled flowers that display a bewildering array of tints. Graham Thomas mentions cerise, magenta, purple, violet, lilac-grey, soft brown and lilac-white, and all these colours are to be found, depending on the stage of development of the flower and the prevailing weather conditions. Perhaps it is simpler to say the overall colour effect is lilac, violet and silvery-grey. It forms a sturdy shrub with ample foliage, and will grow to about 4ft. in height. For some years now a rose named 'Jenny Duval' has been distributed by nurserymen, including ourselves. It is now generally agreed that this is the same as 'Président de Sèze'. To those who have known this rose under both names, it may seem strange that we have taken so long to arrive at this conclusion. My only defence is that this rose is so various and ever-changing in its colour that the confusion between the two was understandable. I have had more than one not inexperienced rose enthusiast come to me with what they thought was yet another entirely different sport, and this too has turned out to be the same variety. The truth is that 'Président de Sèze' differs so widely according to the conditions under which it is grown that it seldom looks the same on any two occasions. There is a pleasing fragrance. Nothing is known of its origin, but Graham Thomas obtained it from Babbink & Atkins of New Jersey and distributed it in Britain.

ROSA MUNDI (*Rosa gallica versicolor*). This is a striped sport of 'Officinalis', having all the virtues of that excellent rose, to which it is similar in every respect except colour. This is palest blush-pink, clearly striped and splashed with light crimson which provides an attractively fresh appearance. Occasionally a flower will revert to the colour of its parent. It has the same strong bushy growth, and flowers in the same

happy profusion as 'Officinalis', providing a wonderful massed effect. Both roses make fine low hedges — indeed it would be hard to find better roses for this purpose. The date of this rose is not known, but it certainly goes back to the sixteenth century and earlier. Like its parent it will make a 4 by 4ft. shrub.

SURPASSE TOUT. Large full, tightly-packed flowers of light rose-crimson, turning with age to cerise-pink. The petals reflex and there is a button eye at the centre. The growth is strong and bushy, the height about 4ft. Strong fragrance. In existence before 1832. See page 30.

TRICOLORE DE FLANDRE. Large, fairly full white flowers heavily striped with shades of lilac, purple and crimson. The growth is short, about 3ft. in height, but vigorous with plentiful smooth foliage. Fragrant. Bred by Van Houtte (Belgium), 1846.

TUSCANY. A rose which can be compared with 'Officinalis' and 'Rosa Mundi', both in its habit of growth and for its excellence as a garden shrub. It has fairly large semi-double flowers of the darkest maroon-crimson; these open wide, with bright golden stamens lighting up the centre. It forms a sturdy bush of 4ft. and, on its own roots, will spread freely if permitted. The foliage is dark green. We do not know the age of this beautiful variety, but it probably goes back a very long way. There is only a slight fragrance. It was once known as the 'Old Velvet Rose' — the herbalist Gerard, writing in 1597, mentions a 'Velvet Rose', and it is likely that this is the same variety.

TUSCANY SUPERB. A larger version of 'Tuscany', with taller more vigorous growth to about 4ft. in height, larger, more rounded leaves and larger flowers with more numerous petals. It is in fact 'more' everything, while remaining at the same time very similar in its general character and colouring; the stamens are partially obscured, as these tend to be hidden by the extra petals. Its origins are not known, but it was recorded by Paul in 1848. It must have been either a sport or a seedling from 'Tuscany' — probably the latter.

TUSCANY SUPERB, *Gallica Rose. An excellent garden shrub.*

Damask Roses

The Damask Rose, like the Gallica, dates back to ancient times. It is said to have been widely grown by the Persians and brought to Europe by the Crusaders. S.F. Hamble gives the credit for this to a Robert de Brie whom, he says, brought it to his castle in Champagne at some time between 1254 and 1276, whence it was distributed throughout France and later brought to this country.

According to Dr. Hurst, the Damask Rose originated from a natural hybrid of the Gallica Rose and a wild species known as *Rosa phoenicea*. The latter rose is a sprawling shrub or climber of no particular garden merit, bearing corymbs of small white flowers. We thus have two widely differing parents, and it is therefore not surprising that this family is itself somewhat diverse in its nature. In general Damask Roses are taller than Gallicas, perhaps 5ft. in height, more lax in growth, with more and larger thorns. The leaves are elongated and pointed, of a greyish-green colour and downy on the underside. Where there are hips these will usually be long and thin. The flowers are nearly always a lovely clear pink and have not inherited any of the purplish-red shades of their Gallica parent. They are often held in nicely poised sprays. The Damasks are usually strongly fragrant, the very name being synonymous with this quality. They bring elegance to the rose, both in leaf and general habit of growth.

Closely related to these roses is the Autumn Damask. This is a rose of great antiquity. It is not, perhaps, of the highest value for the garden, but is of great interest to the student of roses in that it was the only rose to have the ability to repeat flower prior to the introduction of the China Rose late in the eighteenth century. It is of equal interest for its very long history. Dr. Hurst tells us that it is first noted in the Greek island of Samos towards the end of the tenth century B.C., where it was used in the cult of Aphrodite. It was later introduced to mainland Greece and then to Rome where it continued to play a part in ceremonies connected with Venus. In the first century B.C. Virgil in *The Georgics* mentions the rose which flowers twice a year, and this was no doubt the Autumn Damask. This is a rather prickly shrub, with the leaves running right up to and clustering around the flowers. It has an unsophisticated charm and the typical Damask fragrance. It eventually led to the Portland Roses, through which it played an important part in the development of repeat-flowering roses about which I write in the next chapter.

CELSIANA. A typical Damask Rose, with fine, graceful grey-green foliage. The flowers are large, opening wide, semi-double, and of a soft pink colour that later fades to blush, with a central boss of golden stamens. They are held in delicately poised sprays, and the petals have the appearance of crumpled silk. There is a strong fragrance. Height approximately 5ft. I place this rose high on any list of Old Roses. Known to have been in existence before 1750. See pages 38 and 39.

GLOIRE DE GUILAN. In 1949 this rose was collected by Nancy Lindsay from Iran, where it is used for the making of attar of roses. It forms a loose sprawling shrub with apple-green leaves. The flowers are cupped at first, later becoming flat and quartered. Their colour is a pink of unusual clarity and purity, and they are very fragrant. I have found it to be particularly resistant to disease. Height 4ft. See page 43.

HEBE'S LIP (*Rubrotincta*). A modest rose but not without its attractions. It has cupped semi-double flowers, with red-tipped petals that give it its name. The growth is short and thorny with fresh green foliage. Height 4ft. It is probably of hybrid origin, perhaps Damask x *Rosa eglanteria*. See page 39.

ISPAHAN ('Pompon des Princes'). A very fine shrub which begins to flower early and continues over a long period. The flowers are large and very full, opening flat, and of a rich warm pink that does not fade. A good cut flower, lasting well in water. It has a glorious fragrance. Height 5ft. In cultivation before 1832. See page 39.

KAZANLIK (*Rosa damascena trigintipetala*). One of the roses grown at Kazanlik in Bulgaria for the production of attar of roses. The blooms are pink and of no great merit, but it does form a graceful and typical Damask shrub, and has, as might be expected, a rich fragrance. Height 5 or 6ft. Probably of great antiquity.

LA VILLE DE BRUXELLES. Exceptionally large full-petalled blooms of a clear rich pink. When fully open the petals reflex at the edges, leaving a slightly domed centre filled with small petals. A truly luxurious flower of fine quality. The foliage is large and plentiful, pale green in colour and of typical Damask shapeliness. Its growth is upright but often weighed down by the heavy blooms, particularly in moist weather. Rich fragrance. Height 4ft. Vibert (France), 1849.

LEDA. Milk-white flowers with the slightest suggestion of pink. As they open they develop a picot effect, the rim of the petals becoming stained with crimson, so giving rise to its other name the 'Painted Damask'. The blooms are full petalled, reflexing to reveal a button

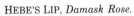
HEBE'S LIP, *Damask Rose.*

ISPAHAN, *Damask Rose.*

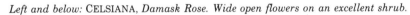
Left and below: CELSIANA, *Damask Rose. Wide open flowers on an excellent shrub.*

centre. Although not perhaps quite so exciting as the description implies, it is a pretty rose with good foliage. Slight fragrance. Height 3ft. Prior to 1827.

MADAME HARDY. One of the classic Old Roses — only a few others can approach it for the sheer perfection of its flowers. They are not very large, of pretty cupped formation at first, later becoming flat and finally reflexing. There is the slightest hint of blush in the early stages, but later they become a pure glistening white, while at the centre a small green eye adds to the attraction. They are held in nicely poised clusters, and are fragrant with just a hint of lemon. It will grow to about 5ft. and is reasonably strong, although it will repay more generous treatment with manure and fertiliser. The foliage is pale green. We cannot be sure of its origin, though it is obviously not pure Damask, the leaves and growth showing signs of Centifolia influence. Bred in 1832 by Hardy (who had charge of the Empress Josephine's famous rose collection at Malmaison) and named after his wife. See page 42.

MADAME ZOETMANS. A charming rose not often seen but gaining in popularity. Its flowers are of medium size, fully double, of cupped formation at first, opening to reveal a button eye. Their colour is white, tinted with blush at the centre, and they are borne on graceful growth on a nice bushy plant with fresh green foliage. Height 4ft. Bred by Marest (France), 1830.

MARIE LOUISE. A lax-growing shrub vying with 'La Ville de Bruxelles' for the splendour of its flowers. These are unusually large and full, of deep pink with the petals reflexing, and very fragrant. The sheer weight and quantity of the flowers often weighs down the branches to the ground. The height is about 4ft. with plentiful large foliage. Here we have a rose that might well be encouraged to flop over a low retaining wall. Raised at Malmaison, 1813. See page 14.

OEILLET PARFAIT. A compact, twiggy shrub of 3 to 4ft., with small pale green leaves. The flowers open flat with numerous petals of warm pink colouring, later reflexing almost to a ball. There is also a striped Gallica of the same name.

OMAR KHAYYAM. This rose is perhaps of more historic interest than garden value. It is the rose that grows on the poet Edward Fitzgerald's grave at Boulge, Suffolk, and which was itself first raised from seed from a rose on Omar Khayyam's grave at Nashipur in Persia. The flowers are soft pink, fragrant, of medium size, and quartered, with a button eye. Grey-green downy foliage. Height 3ft. About 1893.

PETITE LISETTE. A miniature-flowered Damask carrying small bunches of perfect little flowers, each well filled with clear pink petals. It has small, neat, downy grey-green foliage, and forms an excellent well-rounded shrub of 3 to 4ft. in height. Bred and introduced by Vibert (France), 1817.

QUATRE SAISONS (*Rosa damascena bifera*, the 'Rose of the Four Seasons'). This is the repeat flowering Autumn Damask I mentioned in the introduction to this section. The flowers are clear pink, loosely double, with long sepals and a powerful fragrance. It has rather spreading growth and greyish-green foliage. An ancient and most historic rose. Height 5ft.

SAINT NICHOLAS. A recent addition to this very old class, which occurred as a chance seedling, in 1950, in the garden of The Hon. Robert James, at Richmond, Yorkshire. The flowers are semi-double, opening flat, and of a rich pink colour with yellow stamens. It forms a short prickly bush of 5ft. in height, with good, dark green foliage. See page 42.

YORK AND LANCASTER (*Rosa damascena versicolor*). A tall shrub, with clear downy grey-green foliage, which carries its flowers with elegance in dainty open sprays. These are unusual in that they may be pink or almost white, or a mixture of both, the white being flecked with pink and vice versa, all these variations being found on one shrub at the same time. The individual flowers are informal and semi-double, usually exposing their stamens. It is not a dramatic shrub, but it does have a certain airy elegance. The story that the two factions in the Wars of the Roses each took a bloom from a bush of this rose — a red and a white — is probably not true. The roses of the two houses were in fact more likely to have been *R. gallica officinalis* and '*R. alba semi-plena*, although there is no firm historical evidence for this. It is important to obtain bushes from correct stock, as the flowers can easily revert to pink. Fragrant. Height 5ft. Known to be in existence before 1550.

Right: GLOIRE DE GUILAN, *Damask Rose. Beautiful flowers of a very clear pink — here a little faded.*

SAINT NICHOLAS, *a rich pink Damask Rose.*

MADAME HARDY, *Damask Rose. One of the most perfect flowered of all Old Roses.*

Alba Roses

The Alba Roses form another very old group. In existence in classical times and probably brought to Britain by the Romans, they were widely grown in the Middle Ages, no doubt mainly for medicinal purposes, and appear in many paintings of that period. The other classes of ancient roses have a great deal in common and a casual observer might see them as all of one type, but this is not the case with the Albas which are quite distinct. It is generally agreed that they are the result of natural hybridization between the Damask Rose and *Rosa canina,* the Dog Rose of our hedgerows, or at least a species closely allied to it. A cursory inspection of the growth of the Dog Rose will show its close affinity to Alba Roses. As with other Old Roses many of its varieties appear to be the result of further hybridization with roses of other classes.

The Albas form a small but important group which includes some of the best and most beautiful of the Old Roses. Their growth is larger than that of the other old classes, often 6ft. or more in height, and it is no doubt for this reason that they were formerly known as Tree Roses. The flowers, as the name suggests, are rather limited in their colour range, being restricted to white, blush and pink, but they have a delicacy and refinement that is hard to match elsewhere. Their foliage is frequently grey-green in colour, and this tones well with their soft tints and provides an excellent contrast with other roses and plants. They nearly all have a pleasing and characteristic fragrance.

The delicate appearance of the flowers is in sharp contrast to the undoubted toughness of the plant which will grow under difficult conditions. Albas are, in fact, among the most easily grown of all roses, and even in partial shade will do better than most others, although no roses really like such conditions. Whenever we are asked at our nursery for roses that will grow in partial shade, it is always to these we first turn. They are ideal for the border or as individual specimens, or for planting in the more wild areas of the garden. They will also form a particularly fine hedge, different varieties of similar stature mingling together most satisfactorily. The taller varieties may be trained as climbers and they are quite happy when grown on a north wall.

ALBA MAXIMA ('Great Double White', the 'Cheshire Rose', the 'Jacobite Rose'). An ancient rose known to have existed in classical times, it has been grown in cottage gardens in this country for many centuries, where it lives on almost indefinitely, continually renewing its growth. It is not uncommon to see this variety growing, apparently wild, in hedgerows, such plants marking the place where a cottage once stood but which has now long since gone and only the rose remains. There can be no better testimony to its durability. Surely this must be one of the longest lived of all roses? It forms a tall if rather top-heavy shrub of 6ft., and although the individual flowers are not particularly distinguished they are most effective in the mass. Fully double, they are blush-pink at first but soon turn to creamy-white. Strong fragrance. See page 46.

ALBA SEMI-PLENA. Said to have been the 'White Rose of York', this is a luxuriant shrub with fine grey-green foliage and elegant shapely growth. The flowers are large, almost single, symmetrical in outline and milky-white in colour, with a large boss of stamens. They are followed in the autumn by typical Dog Rose hips. This is one of two roses cultivated at Kazanlik, Bulgaria, for the production of attar of roses. In every way a first class garden shrub. Very fragrant. Height 6ft. See page 47.

AMELIA. Here we have a smaller shrub than is usual among Albas. It bears large strongly fragrant pure pink semi-double flowers with pronounced golden stamens. Its height is about 4ft. Bred by Vibert (France), 1823.

BELLE AMOUR. A strong shrub, 6ft. in height, bearing clusters of semi-double slightly cupped flowers of a soft salmon-pink — a shade almost unique among Old Roses. These have a myrrh fragrance which suggests this rose may have some Ayrshire 'Splendens' in its make up. It was originally discovered growing on the wall of a convent at Elboeuf, Normandy.

CELESTIAL ('Céleste'). A modest rose, much treasured for the charm and delicacy of its exquisitely scrolled buds and semi-double flowers of lovely soft pink colouring. These are not large and have yellow stamens. The blooms are beautiful against the grey-green of the typically Alba foliage, and have a sweet fragrance. However the growth is anything but delicate, forming a robust shrub which, in our experience, should not be pruned too severely, otherwise it tends to make growth at the expense of flowers. It forms a shrub of 5ft. in height by 4ft. across. It is said to have been bred in Holland towards the end of the eighteenth century.

FÉLICITÉ PARMENTIER. At its best this is a most beautiful rose, with perfect quartered flowers very tightly packed with petals of clear fresh

MADAME LEGRAS DE ST. GERMAIN, *Alba Rose. One of the most perfect of the Old Roses.*

ROSA ALBA MAXIMA, *Alba Rose.*

ROSA ALBA SEMI-PLENA, *an excellent shrub for partial shade and difficult positions.*

FÉLICITÉ PARMENTIER, *Alba Rose. Beautifully-formed flowers of delicate colouring.*

pink; these later reflex and fade to cream at the edges. The growth is quite short, about 4ft. in height, but bushy, with many thorns and pale green leaves. It is an excellent rose, but in dry seasons on sandy soil the flowers sometimes fail to open properly; with good management this should not be a problem. Known to have been in cultivation in 1834. See page 47.

MADAME LEGRAS DE ST. GERMAIN. A rose of exceptional beauty. Starting as a prettily cupped bud, it opens to form a perfectly shaped slightly domed flower with many petals. The colour is a glowing white with just a tinge of yellow, and this gives us a hint as to its origins — there has to have been a Noisette somewhere in its breeding. It would be hard to think of a more perfect marriage than Alba and Noisette, although in this case it has led to one weakness: the flowers can be damaged by wet weather. Otherwise it is sheer perfection. The growth is tall and lax, forming a graceful shrub of 6ft. in height, with few thorns and pale green leaves. Fragrant. It can equally well be grown as a Climber. Introduced prior to 1848. See page 46.

MADAME PLANTIER. This is an Alba/Noisette hybrid and, in fact, is sometimes classified as a Noisette. It forms a sprawling mound of graceful growth covered with large clusters of rather small pompon-like blooms against pale green foliage. The colour is creamy-white, lightly tinged with yellow at first, later turning to pure white, and there is a pointed green eye at the centre of each flower. Its sweet and powerful fragrance fills the air. It is equally effective when trained as a Climber, and I have vivid memories of a visit to Sissinghurst Castle and being shown this rose climbing up the trunks of fruit trees where they made a wonderful sight like billowing dresses. The height is 6ft. spreading to 6ft. across. Bred and introduced by Plantier (France), 1835. See page 50.

MAIDEN'S BLUSH (known in France as 'Cuisse de Nymphe' and at other times and in various countries as 'La Royale', 'La Seduisante', 'Virginale', 'Incarnata'). This forms a graceful arching shrub of 5ft. in height with typical grey-green Alba foliage. The flowers are loosely double, of soft blush-pink, the petals reflexing slightly with age and paling towards the edges. They have a delicate fragrance. An old and much loved rose and certainly in existence before the beginning of the sixteenth century. See page 50.

MAIDEN'S BLUSH (small). This has smaller flowers than the above rose and grows to only 4ft. in height. I do not know whether it was a sport or a seedling from 'Maiden's Blush', but it is similar in every respect except size. Raised at Kew in 1797.

POMPON BLANC PARFAIT. An unusual rose and difficult to compare with any other. It has little round buds which open to small, flat, tightly-packed pompon flowers on short thin stems. The flowers are pale lilac-pink in colour and of very neat formation. They appear late in the season and are then produced a few at a time in long succession. The growth tends to be slow to develop, with small grey-green leaves and twiggy, rather stiff, almost reluctant growth, of perhaps 4ft in height. Slight fragrance. Introduced 1876.

QUEEN OF DENMARK ('Koenigin von Danemarck'). Few old roses can equal this for the perfection of its individual blooms. These are prettily cupped in the bud and later develop into a full perfectly quartered, slightly reflexing flower with a button eye at the centre. The colour is a warm rose-pink. Strong fragrance. The growth is comparatively short, perhaps 4 or 5ft. in height, with typical grey-green foliage. Like all Albas it is easily grown, but superb blooms can be obtained with good cultivation. Raised in 1816 by John Booth, who recorded it as a seedling from 'Maiden's Blush', and introduced it in 1826. See page 51.

Old Roses with their soft colours and graceful form are ideal for using in a mixed border.

MADAME PLANTIER, *Alba Rose. An excellent free-flowering shrub or Climber.*

MAIDEN'S BLUSH, *a gracefully arching Alba Rose.*

QUEEN OF DENMARK, *Alba Rose. This is one of the most beautiful of the Old Roses.*

Centifolia Roses

The Centifolias were for a long time thought to be the most ancient of all roses, but subsequent research has proved this to be far from the truth. They are mere children by comparison with the three classes discussed so far. It seems that they evolved over a period extending from early in the seventeenth century to the beginning of the eighteenth century, that they were largely the result of the work of Dutch breeders, and that during the period mentioned some two hundred varieties were known to have been introduced. It is not easy to say exactly how they arose, but Dr. Hurst's work shows that *Rosa gallica, R. phoenicea, R. moschata* and *R. canina* all come into their make up. This would seem to indicate that a Damask/Alba cross might have occurred at some time, although it was probably rather more complex than that. It is likely that a series of crosses took place over a long period, resulting in what came to be regarded as a distinct breed. Centifolias were great favourites with our forefathers who seem to have prized them above all others, and evidence of this is provided by the Dutch and Flemish flower painters who used them in their work more frequently than any other roses.

The typical Centifolia has lax, open, rather lanky growth with a mixture of large and small thorns; the leaves are large, rounded and broadly toothed; the flowers tend to be heavy and globular with numerous petals. In spite of all this Centifolias are seldom clumsy and their luxuriant blooms nod gracefully on their stems. Their colours are, in the main, warm clear shades of pink, which do not normally fade in the sun. There are also a number of varieties of hybrid origin which tend towards crimson and pleasing shades of purple and mauve, as well as one or two whites. They are rightly famous for their rich fragrance.

The Centifolias have a strong tendency to produce sports, and this has resulted in a number of unusual forms. Foremost amongst these are the Moss Roses, but there are also quaint and unusual varieties such as 'Chapeau de Napoléon', 'Bullata' and a number of charming miniatures.

It is sometimes worth while giving some of the more lax-growing varieties a little support to stop them bending too near the ground. Pruning can be rather more severe than with other Old Roses, and should be just enough to keep the bush in order, without losing the grace of their arching growth.

BLANCHEFLEUR. Heavy, full-petalled, creamy-white flowers with a tinge of blush at the centre and red on the tips of the petals. It forms a vigorous 5ft. bush with many thorns and apple-green foliage, and shows signs of hybrid origin. Perhaps a little coarse in appearance for my taste, but it is the only white Centifolia we have. Fragrant. Raised by Vibert (France), 1835.

BULLATA (the 'Lettuce-leaved Rose'). This is probably a sport of 'Centifolia' to which it is similar, with the same cupped flowers and rich fragrance. The difference lies in the leaves, which are excessively enlarged and deeply crinkled, like the leaves of a lettuce. It is perhaps due to the effort of producing such foliage that the flowers tend to be rather inferior to 'Centifolia' and do not always open well. The height is 4ft. An interesting curiosity that seems to have originated in 1801.

CENTIFOLIA (the 'Rose of a Hundred Leaves', 'Rose des Peintres', the 'Provence Rose'). The type from which this group derives its name. Even those who know little or nothing about Old Roses will usually have heard of it by its name of 'Old Cabbage Rose'. To the old herbalists it was the 'Queen of Roses', and indeed it is the most beautiful of the Centifolia Roses with its heavy nodding blooms of warm glowing pink and rich Old Rose fragrance. It has strong, nicely arching growth of about 5ft. The flowers are at their best in warm, dry weather. Prior to 1600. See page 55.

CHAPEAU DE NAPOLÉON (*Rosa centifolia* 'Cristata', 'Crested Moss'). This rose is very similar to 'Centifolia', described above. It is distinguished by the fact that the calyx is greatly enlarged in much the same way as a Moss Rose, giving the bud the appearance of a three-cornered cockade hat. Closer observation will reveal that this is not the same as the 'moss' of a Moss Rose, but what Bunyard describes as 'an exaggerated development of the sepals'. However we describe it, the result is very attractive. Although the open flower is not quite so deep as 'Centifolia', it is otherwise indistinguishable, with the same clear pink colouring. It is said that it was originally found in 1820, growing in the crevice of an old wall at Fribourg in Switzerland. This suggests, rather surprisingly, that it was a seedling, not a sport. There is a rich fragrance. Height about 5ft. Introduced by Vibert (France) as 'Crested Moss', 1826. See page 55.

COTTAGE MAID. A rose which has had many names in its time: 'Belle des Jardins', 'La Rubanée', 'Village Maid', 'Panachée à Fleurs Doubles', 'La Belle Villageoise', 'Dometil Beccard' and 'Dominic Boccardo'. It is

TOUR DE MALAKOFF, *Centifolia Rose. A graceful shrub and one of the most beautiful of the purple shades.*

CHAPEAU DE NAPOLÉON, *Centifolia Rose. Similar to 'Centifolia', but with moss-like growth.*

CENTIFOLIA, *the 'Old Cabbage Rose', fading slightly.*

perhaps more properly known as 'Variegata', but we have chosen 'Cottage Maid' as being rather more picturesque. The flowers are quite large and globular in shape with numerous petals, the colour creamy-white, delicately striped with pale pink. It is a vigorous bushy shrub of 5ft. in height, with dark green foliage and many thorns. Rich fragrance. Introduced by Vibert (France), 1845.

DE MEAUX. A miniature Centifolia which has to be compared with other miniatures of this class — 'Petite de Hollande' and 'Spong'. Each of these is charming in its own way, like the little roses we might expect to see decorating tea cups. They are ideal for very small gardens. In spite of some reports to the contrary I suspect that they are all sports of larger Centifolias. 'De Meaux' forms a bushy, twiggy shrub of 3½ft. in height, with tiny flowers of only a little more than 1in. across, and small light green foliage to match. The flowers open as little miniature cups and develop into small pompon flowers of typical Old Rose pink. It is in every way a charming little shrub. Said to have originated with a man named Sweet in 1789. See page 58.

FANTIN-LATOUR. We do not know the date or origin of this variety, but it is clearly not of pure Centifolia descent. The leaves and growth show signs of China Rose influence. The flowers, however, have much of the character of a Centifolia, being of a nicely cupped shape, the outer petals reflexing as the flower ages to reveal a button centre. The colour is a blush-pink which deepens towards the centre and there is a delicate and pleasing fragrance. It forms an excellent shrub with good broad growth of 5ft. in height. Named, most appropriately, after the great French artist Henri Fantin-Latour, whose finest paintings were nearly all of flowers and whose favourite flower was the rose. In every way a fine shrub. See page 58.

IPSILANTE. A most beautiful rose, producing some of the finest blooms in this group. They are large, of a lustrous warm pink colouring, cupped at first, opening flat and quartered. The growth is shapely with fine foliage, and in my garden it is more disease resistant than any other Old Rose. Rich fragrance. Height 4ft. Introduced 1821.

JUNO. Like 'Fantin-Latour', this rose has more modern affinities and is probably connected with the Bourbons. It bears fragrant globular flowers of soft blush pink, later opening flat to reveal a button eye. The growth is rather lax and about 4ft. in height. In cultivation before 1832.

PAUL RICAULT. A 5ft. shrub of medium vigour. The flowers are deep pink, very full petalled and rather globular, the outer petals later recurving. It has a strong fragrance and is free flowering, the blooms hanging gracefully upon the stem. Raised by Portemer (France), 1845. See page 58.

PETITE DE HOLLANDE ('Petite Junon de Hollande', 'Pompon des Dames', 'Normandica'). This is another pretty miniature, with charming little Centifolia flowers of pure rose-pink. It forms a nice bushy little shrub of 4ft. with small leaves and tiny flowers all to scale. Although all are delightful, it is perhaps the best of the miniature-flowered Centifolias, and there is very little to choose between it and 'De Meaux'. Fragrant. First raised in Holland about 1800. See page 58.

ROBERT LE DIABLE. A lax shrub with dark green leaves and thorny stems. The flowers are purple, shaded with slate-grey and splashed with carmine, providing a most pleasing mixture of colour, particularly in hot weather. Of neat rosette shape, the blooms are not large, the petals reflexing towards the edges. Both foliage and flowers show signs of Gallica influence. Late flowering. Height 4ft.

SPONG. A miniature Centifolia of bushy, branching growth, about 4ft. in height, with typical Centifolia leaves. Its flowers are rich pink, paling a little towards the edges. It is rather less formal than 'De Meaux' and 'Petite de Hollande', and has the bad habit of holding its petals long after the flower has died, which is rather unsightly. This is a pretty little rose, but the least effective of the miniatures. Raised by Spong (England), introduced 1805.

THE BISHOP. A very double flower of rosette formation and unique colouring: cerise-magenta with pale lilac on the reverse of the petals, later becoming slate-grey and parma-violet. In certain lights the blooms appear to be almost blue. Gallica influence is very much in evidence. Fragrant. It has rather erect growth of 4ft. in height.

TOUR DE MALAKOFF. A most beautiful rose which will appeal to those who like the purple shades. The flowers are large, opening wide and slightly cupped and only loosely double, but it is the colouring which is their chief glory — a purplish-crimson tinted with magenta becoming violet and with a few stamens usually to be seen at the centre. It is magnificent at all stages. The growth is excellent, perhaps 6ft. in height, arching broadly to form a rather sprawling shrub. Given suitable support it might well be used as a climber. Raised by Soupert & Notting (Luxemburg), 1856. See page 54.

UNIQUE BLANCHE ('White Provence Unique'). Creamy-white flowers which are nicely cupped at first, later opening rather untidily with a

PETITE DE HOLLANDE, *a pretty miniature-flowered Centifolia Rose.*

FANTIN-LATOUR, *Centifolia Rose.*   PAUL RICAULT, *Centifolia Rose.*

DE MEAUX, *Centifolia Rose. This makes one of the most perfect Standard Roses, but flowers only once in the season.*

button eye. At their best they can be most beautiful, the petals having a lovely silky texture. It has strong (if rather untidy) growth and there is a good fragrance. Height 4ft. Discovered at Needham, Suffolk, 1775.

WHITE DE MEAUX. This is a white sport from 'De Meaux', to which it is similar in every way except that the flowers are white tinged with pink. This may sound attractive, but unfortunately the pink is such that it gives the flowers a rather dirty appearance. It is, nonetheless, worthy of its place.

Moss Roses

The Moss Roses are Centifolias which have developed moss-like growth on their sepals and, in some varieties, a little way down the flower stem. This peculiarity is the result of a sport, or fault, in the plant. Small glandular growth is always present to some extent on the sepals of the flower, and in the case of Moss Roses this has become greatly exaggerated. The result is that the bud is covered in this mossy material, giving a most charming effect. We do not know exactly when this curious phenomenon occurred, but Dr. Hurst quotes various French sources which state that a rose of this nature existed in France at Carcassonne in 1696, where it had been for half a century, having been first brought there by one Freard Ducastrel. The earliest mention of it in England was in 1724, when it was listed in the catalogue of Robert Furber of Kensington. Mossing has probably occurred from time to time before and since; indeed it has been recorded subsequently on at least three other occasions. It has also occurred on an Autumn Damask, giving us the 'Perpetual White Moss'.

The majority of Moss Roses were bred over a short period of time, from approximately 1850 to 1870. Arriving, as they did, comparatively late on the rose scene, they show considerable signs of hybridity; in some varieties there are definite signs of China Rose ancestry. Here we have the first hint of the Modern Rose creeping in on the Old. The result is sometimes a loss of that charm which we so value in Old Roses, the first loss of innocence. Nonetheless, most Moss Roses have a beauty which is different from that of other roses. A Moss Rose bud just opening does have a certain charm that is all its own — in George Bunyard's words, 'a cosiness'; for, as he says, 'cosiness lay at the very centre of Victorian taste'. Indeed, I doubt that any other age would have taken them up quite so enthusiastically. They are often a little more stiff and upright than Centifolias, and there is more variation in quality. It is at this stage in the development of the rose that we have to become a little more selective in our choice of varieties.

Most Moss Roses have inherited the strong fragrance of their Centifolia ancestors and pruning should be as recommended for the Centifolias.

BLANCHE MOREAU. Very double, paper-white flowers, starting as a cup and later becoming flat, with contrasting brown moss. This rose is said to be a cross between 'Comtesse de Murinais' and 'Quatre Saisons Blanc', and it does occasionally flower in the autumn. It is perhaps a little lacking in refinement. The growth is rather slender and tall, up to 6ft. Raised by Moreau-Robert (France), 1880.

CAPITAINE BASROGER. Rather shapeless flowers of cerise-purple, and fairly coarse and ungainly growth which is tall and narrow, about 6ft. Little moss. Raised by Moreau-Robert (France), 1890.

CAPITAINE JOHN INGRAM. Full recurving flowers of dusky maroon-purple later becoming purple and showing a button eye. The buds are only sparsely covered with red moss. It forms a vigorous bushy shrub with dark foliage and many thorns. Fragrant. Height 5ft. Bred by Laffay (France), 1854.

COMTESSE DE MURINAIS. Pretty blush-pink buds enfolded in hard green moss, opening to superb quartered blooms with a button eye and fading to white. The growth is vigorous, tall, and erect, its many thorns and light green foliage suggesting a Damask ancestry. Height 6ft. Fragrant. A most beautiful rose. Bred by Vibert (France), 1843. See page 62.

DUCHESSE DE VERNEUIL. A charming rose of delicate refinement, with flowers of a clear fresh-pink colouring, the petals being slightly paler on the reverse side. It has well mossed buds, good foliage and forms a shapely shrub of 4ft. in height. Bred by Portemer (France), introduced 1856.

GENERAL KLEBER. Pretty buds wrapped in fresh green moss opening to form wide flat flowers with silky petals of soft clear pink and a button eye at the centre. It has good bushy growth, about 4 by 4ft., with light green foliage. One of the most beautiful of the Moss Roses. Fragrant. Bred by Robert (France), introduced 1856.

GLOIRE DES MOUSSEUX ('Madame Alboni'). This variety has the largest flowers of the Moss Roses, and indeed some of the largest flowers of all Old Roses. Its full-petalled blooms open wide and flat, reflex at the edges and have a strong fragrance. Their colour is a soft pink which pales with age. There is ample pale green moss on unusually long sepals. A beautiful flower, that may occasionally be damaged by rain. It forms a strong, rather erect, but not unshapely shrub of 5ft. with thick stems and large, light green leaves. Bred by Laffay (France), 1852.

HENRI MARTIN ('Red Moss'). Long crimson buds with contrasting but rather sparse green moss. The open flower is not very full but of attractive, neatly rounded form, and of an unusually pure crimson for

COMTESSE DE MURINAIS, *a tall-growing Moss Rose with flowers of delicate beauty.*

HENRI MARTIN, *Moss Rose.*   SHAILER'S WHITE MOSS, *Moss Rose.*

JAMES MITCHELL, *Moss Rose.*   MOUSSELINE, *Moss Rose.*

JEANNE DE MONTFORT, *a Moss Rose with plenty of brown moss on the buds.*

a Moss Rose, later becoming purple-crimson. The flowers, which are held daintily on thin, wiry stems on a vigorous shrub of up to 6ft. in height, are followed by red hips. Fragrant. Bred by Laffay (France), 1863. See page 62.

JAMES MITCHELL. A vigorous shrub with small magenta flowers that fade to lilac-pink. The buds are dainty and wrapped in dark moss. It is usually the first Moss Rose to flower. Height 5ft. Raised by Verdier (France), 1861. See page 63.

JAPONICA ('Moussu du Japon'). This rose not only has mossy buds but also moss spreading heavily well down the stem, and even on to the leaves. The blooms are magenta-pink and not very impressive; the foliage has purple and copper tints when young. Really only valuable as a curiosity. Height 3ft.

JEANNE DE MONTFORT. A tall and vigorous Moss Rose of 6 or 7ft. in height. Its flowers are clear pink, not very full, have exposed yellow stamens, and are sweetly scented. The buds have plenty of brown moss on long sepals. Bred by Robert (France), 1851. See page 63.

LITTLE GEM. A miniature variety which has small, flat, pompon flowers of a uniform light crimson, but with very little moss. It forms a low bush, no more than 2ft. in height, with small leaves. Raised by Paul (England), 1880.

LOUIS GIMARD. Large cup-shaped flowers, tightly packed with petals of light crimson. It has deep green foliage and the buds are enclosed in dark moss. Height 5ft. Raised by Pernet Père (France), 1877. See page 67.

MADAME DE LA ROCHE-LAMBERT. Attractive crimson buds with dark moss and long sepals, opening to form flat, shapely, full-petalled flowers of crimson-purple. It makes a good bushy shrub of 4ft. in height and occasionally repeat flowers. Bred by Robert (France), 1851.

MARÉCHAL DAVOUST. One of the most satisfactory Moss Roses, when we consider it as a garden shrub. It flowers freely and has graceful, shapely, rather arching growth, creating a most pleasing overall effect. The buds are attractive, with green-brown moss, and open to form shapely flowers of light crimson tinted with purple and mauve, the petals reflexing to show a button centre and a green eye. Height about 4½ft. Fragrant. Raised by Robert (France), 1853. See page 67.

MOUSSELINE. This rose is often found under the name 'Alfred de Dalmas'. No other Moss repeat flowers quite so well, except perhaps

'Salet', which is a much less attractive rose. The buds of 'Mousseline' are pretty and have green-brown moss, although this is not very plentiful. The open flowers are medium sized, cupped, of a soft flesh-pink and delicately scented. The growth is bushy, about 4ft. in height, with pale green, peculiarly spoon-shaped leaves. It appears to be related to the Autumn Damask, probably 'Quatre Saisons Blanc'. A charming little rose. Height 3ft. Raised by Portemer (France), introduced 1855. See page 63.

NUITS DE YOUNG ('Old Black'). The darkest of all the Moss Roses, having small flowers of rich velvety maroon-purple lit by contrasting yellow stamens, with thin buds wrapped in very dark moss. Its growth is slender and wiry and it has small, dark leaves of an almost purple shade. Careful thinning at pruning time and some feeding will be worth while. Height 5ft. Bred by Laffay (France), 1845. See page 66.

OLD PINK MOSS. It seems certain that this well-known rose was a sport from *Rosa centifolia*. It is a little smaller and less deep in the flower, probably due to the burden of producing moss. Otherwise it has the same warm, rich pink colouring and strong fragrance, as well as the elegance and poise and other good characteristics of its parent. This is probably the original Moss Rose from which the others are descended. Although many varieties have followed it, none have excelled it, either for the beauty of its flowers or its value as a garden shrub. Height 4ft. It probably dates back to 1700.

RÉNÉ D'ANJOU. Pretty buds with brown-green moss opening to beautiful soft pink flowers with a delicious perfume. The foliage is tinted with bronze and it forms a bushy shrub of 4ft. in height. A charming rose. Bred by Robert (France), 1853.

SALET. A repeat-flowering Moss Rose with blooms of a good clear pink, and red moss. Unfortunately it is rather coarse both in flower and growth, although it is the most perpetual in this class. Height 4ft. Bred by Lacharme (France), 1854.

SHAILER'S WHITE MOSS (*Rosa centifolia muscosa alba*, 'Clifton Rose', also often known as 'White Bath'). This is a sport from 'Old Pink Moss', and is similar except for its colour. As one might expect, it is a most attractive rose, with cupped white flowers tinted with blush at the centre when they first open. It is certainly the best white Moss Rose, and indeed one of the most beautiful of the small band of white Old Roses. It forms an excellent shrub of 4ft. in height. Fragrant. Discovered by Shailer, 1788. See page 62.

NUITS DE YOUNG, *the darkest of all the Moss Roses.*

SOUPERT ET NOTTING. A neat little rose, which is rather different to other Mosses. The flowers are quite small, deep lilac-pink, neatly rounded and flat with closely packed petals, and have an attractive formality. The growth is short and bushy, to about 3ft. in height, and it repeat flowers well in the late summer. Although the moss is not very conspicuous, this is a charming rose. Bred by Pernet Père (France), 1874.

WILLIAM LOBB ('Old Velvet Rose'). A tall and vigorous shrub of rather straggly growth, 6 to 8ft. in height, with thorny stems and leaden-green foliage. The flowers are of the most beautiful colouring: a dark crimson-purple turning to lavender and eventually almost to grey, the reverse of the petals being light magenta. They are held in large, open sprays, have plentiful green moss and a strong fragrance. This is an ideal rose for the back of the border, where it will look over the top of other smaller shrubs without showing its rather ungainly growth. It may even, as Graham Thomas suggests, be allowed to scramble into other shrubs, often combining with them to make pleasing colour effects. Raised by Laffay (France), 1855.

WILLIAM LOBB, *a good, reliable, tall Moss Rose for the back of the border.*

MARÉCHAL DAVOUST, *Moss Rose.*   LOUIS GIMARD, *Moss Rose.*

CHAPTER 3
Old Roses II

Towards the end of the eighteenth century something happened which was to change our garden roses for ever. As European travellers and traders began to throw just a little chink of light on the ancient mysteries of China, it was inevitable that plants of that massive land should be brought back to Europe. China is probably the finest source of plant material in the world, and is certainly the home of some of the most beautiful wild roses, having to its credit somewhere in the region of one hundred different species. Before Europeans had seen these in the wild, certain garden hybrids were brought to Britain. These were to be known as the China Roses. Although not particularly striking in appearance, they did have one very important characteristic: the ability to flower not just in early summer but throughout the growing season. They were, as we say, repeat flowering, perpetual flowering, remontant, or recurrent, according to which term you choose. It is interesting and rather surprising that China, in spite of her wealth of wild roses and the fact that she has a very long and honourable tradition of gardens and flowers, never rated the rose very highly. The Chinese were essentially gardeners and their interests centred around peonies, chrysanthemums and other flowers, but only to a small degree the rose, although we do from time to time find it depicted on old pottery and in pictures.

The repeat-flowering characteristic of the China Roses was not entirely new — as we have already seen the Autumn Damask Rose had the same ability which it owed to *Rosa moschata,* itself recurrent flowering from late summer onwards. The ability to flower repeatedly is a phenomenon which does not usually occur in nature and is the result of a sport or mutation in the mechanism of the plant. With one or two exceptions wild roses first of all send up tall non-flowering shoots, and it is only in the next season that the shorter flowering shoots appear on these. In the case of the China Rose something went wrong — or perhaps I should say, for us, went right. A plant appeared which lost its ability to form its main non-flowering stems and produced only flowering stems, with the result that we had a bush on which every stem produced a flower. Having flowered, the rose would normally busy itself with the production of strong stems ready to bear next season's flowers and fruit, but in this case the plant continued to flower without thought for the future. This important fact was, no doubt, noted by some observant and long-forgotten Chinaman, who subsequently propagated the plant. Whoever he was, he made a most important contribution to our garden roses — greater perhaps than anyone has done since, for this discovery doubled or even trebled the period over which we can enjoy roses.

The China Rose originally arrived in this country in four different varieties. These became known as 'Slater's Crimson China', introduced 1792; 'Parsons' Pink China', 1793; 'Hume's Blush China', 1809; and 'Parks' Yellow Tea Scented China', 1824. The origin of these roses is difficult to trace. 'Parks' Yellow' can only have been the result of a cross between *R. gigantea* — which bears the largest flowers of all rose species — and a China Rose.

It may be thought that the arrival of these roses would have caused a great flurry of interest among plant breeders, but this was not, in fact, the case. For one thing, the existing native roses were far more showy by comparison. Before long, however, hybrids with the European roses (those in Chapter 2) did appear, but the gene that provided the repeat-flowering characteristic was what is known as recessive, with the result that the first hybrids were only once flowering. It was only when these hybrids were again crossed with the China Roses that perpetual-flowering varieties began to appear and the revolution began. From then on things moved apace and the rose has never looked quite the same again.

This revolution was not confined to the repeat-flowering characteristic alone. The China Rose, with its connection with *R. gigantea,* was an entirely different rose. Whereas the European roses tended to have rough-textured leaves and many thorns, the China Roses had smooth leaves and few thorns. Moreover, their whole character was different. This provided great opportunities but, as is so often the case with such opportunities, also certain dangers. These we shall be discussing later.

'Slater's Crimson China' brought the richer and purer reds we now find in many roses. Previously the crimsons invariably turned to purple and mauves, though often with pleasing effect. 'Parks' Yellow' gave us the larger, thicker, more waxy petals of *R. gigantea.* It also provided the Tea Rose scent and tints of yellow, though not a rich yellow.

As China blood became mingled with that of the Gallicas and Damasks a great variety of new roses appeared, most of them with the ability to flower repeatedly, if not always well at least to some extent.

In this chapter we cover the various classes which, while showing signs of having a strong China influence, still bear flowers with much of the character of the truly Old Rose, and can generally be described as shrubs rather than bushes. These include the Portland Roses, the Bourbons, the Hybrid Perpetuals and the Tea Roses, as well as the China Roses themselves, although there is some doubt as to the inclusion of China blood in the Portlands — at least in the early varieties. All these groups tend to have foliage nearer the China Roses than the European roses; they are, in fact, beginning to look more like the Modern Roses, but the flowers still retain the full, open Old Rose formation.

This second part of the Old Rose history is rather in the nature of an unfinished story. The flower formation and shrub-like growth of the Old Roses were soon to be superseded by the pointed buds and low bush growth of the Hybrid Teas before breeders had brought Old Roses to their full potential. It was unfortunate that the development of the two types was not allowed to continue side by side, but it was not to be. Nonetheless, we have here some roses of real value which it would be a great shame to lose. Happily, as things stand at the moment, there is very little likelihood of this happening.

As regards cultivation, it must be borne in mind that these roses are repeat flowering and therefore require more careful attention due to their greater productivity. Soil conditions should be better and manuring more generous; spraying becomes more necessary. The older once-flowering roses can often be planted and more or less forgotten; this is not possible with repeat-flowering roses if we want to obtain worthwhile results.

Now that we are dealing with repeat-flowering shrubs, pruning takes on a greater significance. It is usual to recommend that pruning be done in March, but there is a lot to be said for pruning in December. This has the advantage that the young shooting buds will not be cut away and thus force the plant to start again. The result of December pruning is that flowers appear earlier in the year, leaving the rose plenty of time to produce its second crop, and this before the soil may have dried out. Early pruning can be particularly important in more northerly areas where the seasons are shorter. These roses, being of a shrubby nature, are frequently slow in flowering again. Strong main shoots should be pruned by about one third of their length, while short side shoots should

MADAME ISAAC PEREIRE, *Bourbon Rose. A sumptuous beauty, particularly good in autumn.*

be pruned to two or three eyes. At the same time it will be necessary to remove old and dying growth completely, while always trying to create a nice shapely shrub.

China Roses

China Roses differ in character to most other garden roses; even to those unnumbered masses that are their heirs. They are altogether lighter in growth. This is perhaps because they are diploid, whereas the majority of garden roses are tetraploid; that is to say their cells contain two sets of chromosomes, whereas it is more usual to have four sets, resulting in larger cells and therefore heavier growth. China Roses have airy, twiggy growth, and rather sparse foliage, with pointed leaves, like a lighter version of a Hybrid Tea. Both growth and leaves are often tinted with red when young. The flowers are not showy, nor are they particularly shapely, but they do have a certain unassuming charm. They have an exceptional ability to repeat their flowering, and are seldom without blooms throughout the summer. Their colours are unusual in that they intensify with age, rather than pale, as is the case with European roses.

Till recently the origins of the China Rose remained a mystery. We know of the four original varieties described in the introduction to this chapter, but the wild form eluded us. Although I cannot at this stage be certain, it would appear that this rose has now been found by Mr. Mikinori Ogisu of Tokyo, in the Chinese Province of Sichuan. A photograph of this rose appeared in the Royal National Rose Society's Journal, *The Rose,* in September 1986, together with an article by Graham Thomas. Mr. Ogisu describes it as growing into trees to a height of up to 10ft., and bearing flowers of 2 to 2½ ins. wide, which vary in colour from pink to crimson — the colour being darker in regions of higher altitude. Previously, this rose had been seen by Dr. Augustine Henry in 1884, who described it in *The Gardener's Chronicle* in 1902, where it was illustrated with a drawing. The species is known as *R. chinensis* var. 'Spontanea'. It will be of enormous interest for all students of the rose to see this species when it eventually comes to this country.

The China Roses of our gardens vary considerably according to the conditions under which they are grown. In an open position in this country they will not usually reach much more than 2 or 3ft. in height, although in more favourable areas they will grow much taller. In countries with warmer climates they will make quite large shrubs of 6ft. and more. As to position, it is best to select a more sheltered corner of the garden, perhaps with the protection of a south facing wall which is shielded from the wind. Here they will grow much nearer their full potential. Having said all this, China Roses are not really tender and can be relied on to withstand all but the very hardest winters in the British Isles.

Their light growth and dainty flowers make them particularly suitable for mixing with other plants, especially where something heavier and more robust might be out of place. China Roses require fertile soil, or at least soil that has been well manured, but unlike other roses mentioned in this chapter they dislike hard pruning, and this should usually be done only to maintain the shape of the shrub and to remove dead and ageing growth.

COMTESSE DU CAYLA. A dainty little shrub of 3ft. in height with almost single flowers of varying shades of coppery-pink, eventually becoming salmon-pink with yellow tints at the base of the petal. The foliage is purplish-bronze when young. Tea Rose scent. Raised by P. Guillot (France), 1902.

CRAMOISI SUPÉRIEUR. Small, cupped, fragrant flowers of a clear unfading crimson, produced in small clusters. The growth is short and twiggy, about 3ft. in height in a warm situation. There is also a good climbing form, 'Cramoisi Supérieur Grimpante'. Bred and introduced by Coquereau, 1832.

FABVIER ('Madame Fabvier', 'Colonel Fabvier'). A small low-growing plant of about 1ft. in height, rather similar in habit to a Polyantha Rose. The flowers are small and bright scarlet with a white streak in their petals. It is constantly in bloom and the petals fall before they fade, giving an effect of continuing brilliance. Laffay (France), 1832.

HERMOSA. This shows all the signs of being a China Rose hybrid. We do not know what the other parent was, but certainly it is an excellent little rose. 'Hermosa' has something of the appearance of a Bourbon Rose, but it is smaller in all its parts and more delicate in appearance. The growth is branching and more sturdy than most China Roses, bearing small lilac-pink flowers of a pretty cupped formation. They are borne with admirable continuity throughout the summer. Slight fragrance. Bred and introduced by Marcheseau (France), 1840. See pages 74 and 77.

LE VÉSUVE ('Lemesle'). Dainty scrolled buds of Tea Rose appearance, soft creamy-pink in colour, gradually deepening with age and finally taking on tints of carmine. The flowers have a Tea Rose fragrance and are produced continually on a branching twiggy bush which will, given

OLD BLUSH CHINA, *a good garden shrub.*

HERMOSA, *a China Rose with small flowers.*

MUTABILIS, *a China Rose assorting well with delphiniums and herbaceous geraniums.*

LE VÉSUVE, *a China Rose with Tea-like buds.*

a warm sheltered position, achieve 5ft. in height, although 3ft. would be more usual under average conditions. Introduced by Laffay (France), 1825.

MADAME LAURETTE MESSIMY. Long slender buds with only a few petals which open quickly. They are salmon-pink at first, shaded copper at the base of the petal, the open flower soon fading. It is the result of a cross between 'Rival de Paestum' and the Tea Rose 'Madame Falcot', and is, in fact, of rather Tea Rose appearance. It will grow to 4ft. in height in a warm position. Bred by Guillot Fils (France), 1887.

MUTABILIS ('Tipo Ideale'). Often incorrectly known as *Rosa turkestanica,* this variety rivals the 'Old Blush China' for its excellence as a garden shrub. Its pointed copper-flame buds open to single copper-yellow flowers of butterfly daintiness, soon turning to pink and finally almost crimson. Given a warm sheltered position near a wall it will form an 8ft. shrub which will probably flower as constantly as any other rose. In more exposed positions it is often quite small and frail in appearance. It would be interesting to know of its origins, but unfortunately this information has been lost. See page 75.

OLD BLUSH CHINA ('Parsons' Pink China'). This is a very good garden shrub, with twiggy but quite robust growth and dainty flowers in small clusters. These are produced continually throughout the summer, starting early and finishing late, and for this reason it was formerly known as the 'Monthly Rose'. The flowers are not large and of a loose informality. They are pale pink in colour, deepening with age. The bush

HERMOSA, *a hardy reliable repeat-flowering China Rose.*

usually grows to about 4ft. in height but may be considerably taller in favourable conditions. I have seen it growing as a 10ft. shrub near to a wall in the warm climate of Pembrokeshire. It has a pleasing fragrance which has been described as being similar to that of a Sweet Pea. Introduced to England 1789. See page 74.

RIVAL DE PAESTUM. Long, pointed buds, tinted blush, opening to semi-double ivory-white flowers elegantly poised on a shrub some 4ft. in height. Sometimes classified as a Tea Rose. Raised by G. Paul, 1863.

SOPHIE'S PERPETUAL. A beautiful rose found in an old garden, named by Humphrey Brooke and reintroduced in 1960. The flowers are quite small, of shapely cupped formation and held in small sprays. Their colour is a deep pink. Strong growth with few thorns and dark green foliage. It will grow into a 6ft. shrub and may be used as a Climber. Of obvious hybrid origin.

VIRIDIFLORA (the 'Green Rose'). In this rose the petals are entirely missing and have been replaced by numerous green sepals giving the effect of a green rose. It is, no doubt, a sport from the 'Old Blush China' to which it is very similar in growth. It is of little value as a garden plant, except as a curiosity, although it may have its uses for inclusion in flower arrangements. Introduced 1855.

ARTHUR DE SANSAL. *Both this and 'Rose de Rescht' are unusually dark Portland Roses, both showing the influence of the Gallica Rose.*

Portland Roses

The Portland Roses were the first family in which the China Rose played a part by passing on its ability to repeat flower. They had only a short period of popularity, for they were soon to be overtaken, first by the Bourbons, and not long after by the Hybrid Perpetuals, but in 1848 there were eighty-four varieties growing at Kew. Today only a handful remain, but they form, nonetheless, a not unimportant class, both for their beauty and as one of the parents of the Hybrid Perpetuals.

The origins of the Portland Roses are shrouded in mystery and writers tend to step lightly over the subject, but we do know that around the year 1800 the Duchess of Portland obtained from Italy a rose known as *Rosa paestana* or 'Scarlet Four Seasons' Rose', and that it was from this rose that the group developed. The Portland Rose was repeat flowering, and was thought to have been the result of a cross between a Gallica Rose and the repeat-flowering Autumn Damask. This is unlikely, although it could easily have been a seedling from such a rose. Hurst seems to have had little to say on the subject, although he does note that Redouté's print of 1817 has the appearance of a China-Damask-French hybrid. I would thus assume Hurst had not seen the growing plant. One would expect that there is some China Rose influence there (probably 'Slater's Crimson China'), although there is not much evidence of this in the plant. If this is so, it may well have inherited the recurrent-flowering characteristic from two different sources. The Portland Rose was sent from England to France where André Dupont, gardener to the Empress Josèphine, named it 'Duchess of Portland', and it was not very long before the French had raised numerous varieties.

Portland Roses are not difficult to recognise. They usually show a strong Damask influence, but they are shorter in growth, perhaps 4ft. in height. The flowers tend to have very little stem so that the leaves are packed closely around the flowers, forming what Graham Thomas describes as a rosette or shoulder of leaves.

ROSE DE RESCHT, *a strong, bushy Portland Rose that repeat flowers well.*

Although they cannot be said to be graceful in growth, being rather upright, Portland Roses are well suited to smaller gardens as they form small, compact shrubs. Their virtue lies in the fact that, though repeat flowering, they still retain much of the character of the truly Old Roses and have a strong Damask fragrance. Their ability to repeat is by no means unfailing and varies according to variety, but most of them can be relied on to provide flowers later in the year, many of them producing particularly beautiful Old Rose blooms.

ARTHUR DE SANSAL. A compact, upright shrub with ample foliage, the attractive buds opening to form flat, neatly-shaped very double dark crimson-purple flowers, paler on the reverse side of the petals. There is usually a button eye at the centre of the flower. Richly fragrant. Height 3ft. Raised by Cartier (France), 1855. See page 78.

BLANC DE VIBERT. This variety bears prettily-cupped, many-petalled white flowers with a strong fragrance. It forms an upright bush with ample pale green Damask Rose foliage. Height 3ft. Raised by Vibert (France), introduced 1847.

COMTE DE CHAMBORD. Very full quartered flowers of rich clear pink with a powerful Damask Rose fragrance. The growth is strong and rather upright, about 4ft. in height, with ample foliage, the leaves coming all the way up to the flower in true Portland style. Here we have a rose that retains the true Old Rose character, while at the same time repeat flowering well. One of the best and most beautiful of this class. Raised by Moreau-Robert (France), introduced 1860.

DELAMBRE. A compact bush, bearing full-petalled deep pink flowers against ample dark green foliage. Height 3ft. Bred by Moreau-Robert (France), 1863.

INDIGO. A beautiful dark purple Portland Rose with large flowers. The growth is upright and vigorous. Height 4ft. Circa 1830.

JACQUES CARTIER. Very similar to 'Comte de Chambord', but its shapely full-petalled flowers have, if anything, a little more refinement, although it is not such a good repeat flowerer. It has the same clear pink colouring, fading a little with age, and a button eye at the centre. The growth is compact and erect with light green Damask Rose foliage. Rich fragrance. Height 3½ft. Raised by Moreau-Robert (France), introduced 1868. See page 83.

JAMES VEITCH. This is a superb variety, with lovely purple flowers shaded with slate-grey – truly beautiful colouring. It is a vigorous

COMTE DE CHAMBORD, *one of the most beautiful Portland Roses.*

little plant which repeat-flowers well. It is obviously a Portland/Moss cross, but there is little sign of moss on the buds. Due to its habit growth, I think it is as well placed here. Height 3ft. Verdier 1865.

MARBRÉE. Deep purple-pink flowers mottled with a paler pink and opening flat. The growth is strong and tall for a Portland, with plentiful dark green foliage. Slight fragrance. Height 4ft. Raised by Robert et Moreau (France), 1858.

PERGOLÈSE. Medium-sized, fully double fragrant flowers of a purple-crimson which fades to mauve as they age. They are produced in small clusters on a bushy upright shrub with ample dark green foliage. Height 3ft. Raised by Robert et Moreau (France), introduced 1860.

ROSE DE RESCHT. A shapely, bushy shrub that has quite small neatly-formed very double flowers with closely-packed petals. The purplish-crimson blooms are nicely placed on short stems against ample rough-textured deep green foliage. There are signs of Gallica Rose influence both in flower and leaf, but the fact that it produces a second crop of flowers suggests its place is in this class. Fragrant. Height 3ft. Brought to England by Miss Nancy Lindsay from Iran or France. See page 79.

ROSE DU ROI ('Lee's Crimson Perpetual'). An interesting little rose which has had a great influence on our Modern Roses, being the channel through which we obtained the clear red colouring, first of all in the Hybrid Perpetuals, and from them in the Hybrid Teas of the present day. It is a short rather spreading bush and not particularly robust. The flowers are loosely double, crimson mottled with purple. Strong fragrance. It repeats well and is, all in all, a worthwhile rose in its own right. Raised by Lelieur (France), introduced by Souchet, 1815.

ROSE DU ROI À FLEURS POURPRÉS ('Roi des Pourpres', 'Mogador'). Said to be a sport from 'Rose du Roi', its appearance casts some doubt on this. It is a pretty little rose with loosely formed purple flowers. Of spreading growth, it may achieve about 3ft. under suitable conditions. Introduced 1819.

JACQUES CARTIER, *one of the most charming of the Portland Roses.*

Opposite: THE PORTLAND ROSE, *very influential in the development of the rose.*

THE PORTLAND ROSE (the 'Scarlet Four Seasons' Rose'). This forms an excellent bushy and rather spreading shrub of 3ft. in height with ample foliage. The flowers are semi-double opening wide and of light crimson colouring with conspicuous yellow stamens. A good garden shrub both in summer and autumn. Strong Damask fragrance.

Bourbon Roses

The origins of the Bourbon Rose make a fascinating story and illustrate very well how the various movements in the developments of the early roses always happened by chance. Such happenings sometimes occur in what seem to be the most unlikely places. These roses take their name from l'Île de Bourbon, a small island near Mauritius in the Indian Ocean, now known as Réunion. It is said that farmers of this island were in the habit of planting both the Autumn Damask and the 'Old Blush China' together as hedges. With so many of these roses growing in close proximity there was always a chance that a hybrid would arise, and this, in fact, is what happened. The Parisian botanist Bréon found a rose growing in the garden of a man named A.M. Perchern. This rose was intermediate between the Autumn Damask and the 'Old Blush China' and had been grown in the island for some years under the name 'Rose Edward'. Bréon sent seed of this rose to his friend Jacques, gardener to King Louis-Philippe, and from this seed a rose called 'Rosier de l'Île de Bourbon' was raised. It was distributed in France in 1823 and two years later in England. Not much is known about the early development of these roses, for breeding was then still confined to the chance collection of seed, but we can be sure that several other roses played a part in their development.

The Bourbons represent the first real step towards the Modern Roses. Their flowers still retain the character of the Old Roses with their strong fragrance, and they still have shrubby growth, but their leaves and stems begin to look more like those of the Hybrid Tea, and they are nearly all repeat flowering. Thus we have something of the best of both worlds. They are usually of robust growth and some highly desirable roses are to be found among them.

With Bourbons pruning becomes more important, particularly if we are to take advantage of their ability to flower a second time. Side shoots should be pruned back to three eyes, and strong main shoots reduced by one third. As the years go by, ageing and dead growth should also be removed. A liberal mulching with farmyard manure or compost, and an application of a rose fertilizer in March and again after the first crop of flowers will greatly improve the results. The removal of flowers immediately after they die is also important.

ADAM MESSERICH. A late arrival on the scene. One of its parents was a Hybrid Tea, and this shows up in the rather modern appearance of its growth and foliage — it might be argued that it is not a Bourbon at all. However, this need not worry us as it is a good shrub which may also be grown as a Climber or pillar rose. It is very vigorous, sending up long slightly arching almost thornless growth from the base of the plant. The flowers are large, semi-double, slightly cupped in shape and of a deep warm pink. The fragrance is strong, with a somewhat fruity, some say raspberry, flavour. It flowers freely in early summer but there are only occasional blooms later. Height 5ft. Bred by P. Lambert (Germany), introduced 1920.

BOULE DE NEIGE. A slender upright shrub of perhaps 5ft. in height, its neat dark green foliage betraying its partly Tea Rose ancestry. The flowers are held in small clusters, and its small, round, crimson-tinted buds open to the most perfectly formed creamy-white blooms of posy freshness, the petals gradually turning back on themselves almost forming a ball. Add to this a strong fragrance and we have one of the most charming white Old Roses. Bourbon 'Blanche Lafitte' x the Tea Rose 'Sappho'. Bred by Lacharme (France), 1867. See page 87.

BOURBON QUEEN, *a Bourbon Rose with a strong fragrance.*

COMMANDANT BEAUREPAIRE, *a striped and flecked Bourbon Rose*

BOURBON QUEEN ('Queen of the Bourbons', 'Reine des Îles Bourbon'). A rose frequently found surviving in old gardens after many years. It may be grown either as a tall rather open shrub of up to 6ft. in height, or as a Climber; on a wall it can achieve 10 to 12ft. The flowers are cupped and rather loosely formed with exposed stamens and crinkled petals. In colour they are medium pink veined with deeper pink paling towards the edges. Strong fragrance. Raised by Mauget (France), introduced 1834. See page 85.

COMMANDANT BEAUREPAIRE ('Panachée d'Angers'). The three Bourbon Roses with striped flowers — 'Commandant Beaurepaire', 'Honorine de Brabant' and 'Variegata di Bologna' — are all rather similar. This one is notable for the lovely mixture of colours in its flowers: carmine pink flecked and striped with mauve, purple, scarlet and pale pink, and this so variously that they might be described in a dozen different ways. These colours are at their best in cool weather, as they tend to be rather muddy in very hot sun. The flowers are shallowly

BOULE DE NEIGE, *Bourbon Rose. One of the most perfect white roses.*

HONORINE DE BRABANT, *a Bourbon Rose with a strong fragrance.*

cupped in shape, strongly fragrant and produced very freely. This rose forms a dense leafy bush of strong growth that requires some thinning at pruning time to maintain the quality of its flowers. The height is 5ft. and as much across. It flowers only in early summer. Raised by Moreau-Robert (France), 1874. See page 86.

COUPE D'HÉBÉ. Cupped flowers of pale pink opening full and slightly quartered. The growth is tall, narrow and rather too upright, with light green foliage. It may be grown as a Climber. Bred from a Bourbon hybrid x a China hybrid. Laffay (France), 1840.

HONORINE DE BRABANT. A rose similar to 'Commandant Beaurepaire' but paler in colour — light pink splashed with shades of crimson and purple. It has the advantage over 'Commandant Beaurepaire' in that it repeat flowers quite well, the later flowers often being of better quality in the less intense sunlight of late summer. They are of shallow cupped-shape, opening quartered, with a strong fragrance. The growth is robust and bushy, to about 6ft., with ample foliage. It may also be grown as a Climber.

KRONPRINZESSIN VIKTORIA. This is a sport from 'Souvenir de la Malmaison', see below, and is similar to that rose except that the flowers are creamy-white shaded with pale lemon-yellow. They can easily become discoloured in wet weather, and I have found it to be even less strong than its parent. Unless it is possible to give it exceptional care, it would probably be better not to grow this variety. It originated in 1887 and was introduced by Späth of Berlin.

LOUISE ODIER. A rose out of very much the same mould as 'Reine Victoria', see below, having all its virtues but with more robust and bushy growth. The flowers are beautifully formed, cupped at first, opening flatter and neatly rounded, with each petal precisely in place. Their colour is a lovely warm pink and they have a rich fragrance. Like 'Reine Victoria' it repeats well throughout the summer, and for me it is the most desirable of the recurrent-flowering Old Roses. Height 5ft. I have used this rose for breeding and the results suggest that it has some Noisette in its make up. Raised by Margottin (France), introduced 1851. See page 90.

MADAME ERNST CALVAT. A sport from 'Madame Isaac Pereire' described below. It is similar in every respect, except for the colour which is a medium pink. In my opinion the flowers are a little less happy in this colour than in the deeper shades of its parents, often appearing rather coarse, but as with so many roses we get the occasional perfect flower, particularly in autumn, that makes it all worth while. It has the same strong growth and rich fragrance as 'Madame Isaac Pereire'. Height 6ft. Discovered by Vve. Schwartz (France), 1888.

MADAME ISAAC PEREIRE. A vigorous shrub some 7ft. in height with large, thick, deep green foliage. It bears huge flowers, perhaps 5ins. across. These are cupped at first and quartered on opening, the petals being rolled back at the edges. The colour is a very deep pink shaded with magenta, giving a rich effect, and there is an extremely powerful fragrance. It flowers well in the autumn when it often produces some of its best blooms. A sumptuous beauty, especially when well grown. The parentage is not recorded. Bred by Garçon (France), 1881. See page 71.

MADAME LAURIOL DE BARNY. A most beautiful rose carrying silky richly-fragrant quartered blooms of silvery-pink colouring. They are held in weighty, slightly drooping sprays on a vigorous 6ft. shrub, which may also be trained as a Climber. It has a good crop of flowers in early summer but there are rarely any blooms later. Raised by Trouillard (France), 1868. See page 91.

MADAME PIERRE OGER. A sport from 'Reine Victoria', see below, to which it is similar in every respect except for the colour of the flowers. This is a pale creamy-blush, giving the flowers a refinement exceeding even that of its parent, the beautiful chaliced blooms taking on the appearance of the most delicate porcelain. In very hot weather the colour tends to deepen and harden on the sunny side of the blooms, and in the rain the petals became speckled. The growth is narrow and upright, about 5ft. in height. Fragrant. Discovered by A. Oger (France), 1878. See page 94.

MRS. PAUL. Probably a seedling from 'Madame Isaac Pereire', with which it shares many characteristics. It has large blush-white flowers with a strong perfume. The growth is robust though rather floppy and may require a little support. Plentiful large leaves. Height 5ft. Bred by George Paul (England), introduced by Paul & Sons 1891.

LOUISE ODIER, *Bourbon Rose. A Victorian favourite and one of the most reliably recurrent-flowering of the Old Roses.*

MADAME LAURIOL DE BARNY, *Bourbon Rose. An elegant free-flowering shrub or Climber blooming mainly in the autumn.*

PRINCE CHARLES. Dark purple-crimson flowers turning almost lilac as they age. They are large, flat when open and have petals of a veined and crimped appearance. The growth is strong, about 5ft. in height, with large leaves and few thorns. It has little fragrance and is not recurrent. One of the few dark coloured roses in this class. A sport or seedling of 'Bourbon Queen', introduced 1842.

REINE VICTORIA. In this rose and its sport, 'Madame Pierre Oger', see above, we have two of the most beautiful and best loved roses of this period. They both form slender shrubs of about 5ft. in height, with the blooms elegantly poised above the foliage, indicating a close relationship with China Roses. The flowers are medium sized, chalice shaped rather than cupped, the petals incurving towards the centre to provide a charming enclosed effect and holding their form to the end. The colour is lilac-pink on the outside and paler within. This variety has few rivals among the Old Roses in its ability to flower repeatedly throughout the summer. Unfortunately, as so often happens, along with this goes a greater tendency to blackspot, but no more than we expect in most Modern Roses. Fragrant. Height 4ft. Bred by J. Schwartz (France), introduced 1872. See page 94.

SOUVENIR DE LA MALMAISON. This rose was named in memory of the Empress Josèphine's famous garden at Malmaison and is one of the most popular of the Bourbon Roses. It is available both as a bush and a Climber, but we are only concerned here with the bush which is a short rather spreading shrub of about 3ft. in height. The flowers are a delicate blush-pink which pales a little with age. They are cup-shaped at first, later becoming flat and distinctly quartered to form a large and beautiful flower about 5ins. across, with a fragrance similar to that of a Tea Rose. Raised in 1843 by J. Beluze of France, from a cross between the Bourbon Rose 'Madame Desprez' and a Tea Rose, it has, as we might expect, foliage of rather modern appearance, although the flowers are of truly Old Rose persuasion. It is a reliable repeat flowerer. The growth is rather too short for the flowers, and it is, perhaps, better in its climbing form, of which a description is given in the chapter on Climbing Roses in the companion to this volume – *Modern Roses*. See page 94.

SOUVENIR DE ST. ANNE'S. An almost single sport of 'Souvenir de la Malmaison', found in Lady Ardilaun's garden at St. Anne's, near Dublin. It has not grown very large at our nursery, but I am informed by Graham Thomas, who was responsible for its introduction, that it is capable of forming a fine shrub of 7ft. in height. I suspect it would repay

PRINCE CHARLES, *one of the few dark Bourbon Roses.*

extra generous treatment. The large flowers are a delicate blush-pink colouring and have a nice clean-cut appearance. Rather surprisingly, unlike 'Souvenir de la Malmaison', it has a strong fragrance. Graham Thomas tells me that this stems from *Rosa moschata* in its parentage, in which the fragrance comes from the stamens rather than the petals. Of course, this rose does have stamens, whereas its parent does not. Introduced 1950.

VARIEGATA DI BOLOGNA. The last of our trio of striped Bourbon Roses, and of more recent origin, having been bred in Italy by A. Bonfiglioli as late as 1909. The flowers are white, clearly striped with dark crimson-purple, giving them a purity and freshness that is very appealing particularly in cool weather. They are fully double, cupped in shape, globular at first and quartered when open, and have a strong perfume. This rose has ample foliage and forms a dense shrub of 5 or 6ft., or will climb to 10ft. A distinct and beautiful rose but susceptible to blackspot. See page 95.

ZÉPHIRINE DROUHIN. See the Chapter on Climbing Roses in the companion to this volume

MADAME PIERRE OGER, *Bourbon Rose. Another Victorian favourite.*

SOUVENIR DE LA MALMAISON, *Bourbon Rose.*

REINE VICTORIA, *Bourbon Rose.*

94

VARIEGATA DE BOLOGNA, *a Bourbon Rose of fresh beauty, unfortunately summer flowering only.*

Hybrid Perpetual Roses

We now reach the final stage of development of the rose before arriving at the Hybrid Teas which are, of course, the predominant roses of the present day. It will have been noticed that none of the classes described so far can be said to be in any way pure or clearly defined in so far as their origins are concerned, although they may be quite distinct in their general character and appearance. When we come to the Hybrid Perpetuals this is more than ever true. The Hybrid Perpetuals can best be described as an idea rather than as roses of any definite origins. They are, in fact, an amalgamation of various roses with certain objectives in view — for it is at this stage that large-scale breeding comes into its own — with breeders raising numerous seedlings in the hope of arriving at an ideal. Paul tells us that the French breeder Laffay raised up to 200,000 seedlings annually — more than many large-scale breeders grow today.

It cannot be said that breeding on such a scale led to an all round improvement; indeed there is, to me, a decline in the beauty of the rose since Hybrid Perpetuals first appeared. It is true that, as their name suggests, the Hybrid Perpetuals are repeat flowering, but they are rather clumsy and their growth too tall, narrow and upright, making them unsuitable for use as shrubs in the garden. The nature of their development was in no small degree due to the advent of the rose show which was, during the latter half of the nineteenth century, at the height of its popularity. Roses were exhibited in boxes in which six or more blooms would be placed at equal distances in order to show each of them individually. So keen was the competition that it resulted in a tendency to breed for exhibition only, and the flower as a bud became the exhibitor's ideal. Unfortunately this led to the notion of a rose perfect in bud formation only, while the open bloom, so much appreciated by Old Rose enthusiasts today, was given little regard. At the same time, and equally unfortunately, the breeders' attention was centred on the flower alone; habit of growth was ignored. Such roses were no doubt very fine when seen on the show bench, but as garden plants they left much to be desired.

There are, however, some beautiful Hybrid Perpetuals still surviving, particularly those of earlier date, and many of them well worth a place in the garden. It is these I have included in my list. One or two of them may be a little ungainly, but they are beautiful as cut flowers and do

BARON GIROD DE L'AIN,
*Hybrid Perpetual Rose with
attractive edging.*

BARONESS ROTHSCHILD, *one of the most beautiful Hybrid Perpetuals, and
representative of the other main class of late Victorian roses.*

have at least three virtues: they are nearly all very fragrant, they are recurrent flowering, and many of them have the Old Rose flower formation. In this class we also find varieties of a rich pure crimson colouring, something not found in many other roses before this time.

Hybrid Perpetuals are gross feeders and will repay generous treatment. Some, if left to their own devices, become too tall, and it is best to prune them down by about half their height in order to maintain reasonable proportions and ensure quality and continuity of bloom.

ARRILLAGA. A very late arrival with interesting parentage (*Rosa centifolia* x 'Mrs. John Laing') x 'Frau Karl Druschki', and therefore by no means a pure Hybrid Perpetual, if indeed there is such a thing. It forms a tall shrub, often growing to over 6ft. in height. The flowers are in the Old Rose tradition, soft pink in colour, with a light fragrance. The first flowering is very prolific, but there is only an occasional bloom later in the summer. Bred by Schoener (U.S.A.), introduced 1929.

BARONESS ROTHSCHILD. Large shallowly cupped flowers, frequently of the most perfect formation, the petals later recurving. They are of a soft pink colour, deepening towards the centre. The growth is erect, to 4ft. in height, and thorny, with greyish-green foliage coming close up to the flower in the manner of a Portland Rose to which it is probably closely related. It is free flowering and repeats quite well. This variety produces some of the most beautiful flowers in this section — it is unfortunate that it has little fragrance. A sport of 'Souvenir de la Reine d'Angleterre'. Discovered by Pernet Père (France), 1868. See page 97.

BARON GIROD DE L'AIN. A 'Eugène Fürst' sport, discovered by Reverchon of France in 1897. Unlike many Hybrid Perpetuals it forms a broad shapely shrub which grows strongly without being too upright. It has fine large foliage. The flowers, like those of its parent, are a dark heavy crimson, but with the added and unusual attraction that the petals are neatly edged with a thin line of white. They are large and of shapely cupped formation, and their colour holds well, showing off the dual effect to perfection. It repeats quite well under good conditions and has a rich fragrance. Height 4ft. See page 97.

BARONNE PRÉVOST. Large flowers in the Old Rose tradition, opening flat and quartered with a small button eye. The colour is pale rose-pink. Its growth is strong and very upright, about 4ft. in height. Fragrant. Bred by M. Desprez (France), 1842. See page 100.

DUKE OF EDINBURGH. One of the best of the bright red Hybrid Perpetuals, forming a strong erect bush of about 3ft. in height. The flowers are full, of open incurved formation and fragrant, repeating quite well in the autumn. A hybrid of 'Général Jacqueminot'. Bred by George Paul (England), 1868.

EMPEREUR DU MAROC. This variety is chiefly notable for the richness of its dark velvety maroon-crimson colouring. The flowers are not very large, opening flat, quartered, and well filled with petals which later reflex. Strong fragrance. Unfortunately the growth is rather weak, often resulting in poor flowers, and it requires a high standard of cultivation to produce worthwhile results. Its foliage is similar to that of a Hybrid Tea and is rather sparse. Only slightly recurrent. Height 3ft. A seedling from 'Géant des Batailles'. Bred by Bertrand-Guinoisseau (France), 1858.

EUGÈNE FÜRST. Large globular flowers of rich velvety crimson-purple, paler on the reverse side of the petals. These are borne on a broad well-formed shrub of about 4ft. in height with large foliage. There is a good fragrance. Its breeding is 'Baron de Bonstetten' x an unnamed variety. Bred by Soupert & Notting (Luxemburg), 1875.

FERDINAND PICHARD. A striped rose that can be compared to the striped Bourbon varieties such as 'Commandant Beaurepaire'. Its flowers are pink, striped and splashed with crimson, the pink gradually fading almost to white while the crimson intensifies. They are of medium size, cupped in shape, not very full and fragrant. This rose forms a bushy shrub by the standards of a Hybrid Perpetual and flowers intermittently in late summer after the first crop. One of the best striped roses, as good as its Bourbon rivals, and perhaps the best one for the smaller garden. Height 5ft. It was raised by R. Tanne of France as recently as 1921, and may well be a sport, but from which rose we do not know. See page 105.

FISHER HOLMES. Pointed buds of scarlet and crimson, in the manner of a Hybrid Tea, the colour soon fading. It flowers both in summer and autumn and forms a healthy bush of about 4ft. in height. Fragrant. Thought to be a seedling of 'Maurice Bernardin'. Bred by Verdier (France), 1865. See page 104.

FRAU KARL DRUSCHKI ('Snow Queen', 'Reine des Neiges', 'White American Beauty'). This rose belongs theoretically to the Hybrid Teas, being a cross between the Hybrid Perpetual 'Merveille de Lyon' and the Hybrid Tea 'Madame Caroline Testout', but the growth is so tall, up to 6ft. in height, that it would be misleading to place it anywhere else but here. The flowers, however, which are white with just a hint of lemon, are very close to those of a Hybrid Tea, and even today it is difficult to find a white Hybrid Tea flower that is better than this. It should be pruned as described in the introduction to this section, and will then form a tall, narrow, but slightly arching shrub, ideal for the back of the border. A group of two or three plants will knit together into a more shapely whole and give a more satisfactory effect. The foliage is light green. This is a tough old campaigner, although it may require spraying against mildew. Little or no fragrance. Raised by Lambert (Germany), 1901.

GÉNÉRAL JACQUEMINOT ('General Jack', 'Jack Rose'). An important variety in the development of the Modern Rose and perhaps of more interest for this than for any particular qualities of its own. In fact, most of the red roses of the present day relate back to this variety. It has rich crimson full-petalled flowers, opening rather untidily. The fragrance is particularly strong, and it was perhaps because of this rose and other similar Hybrid Perpetuals that the idea grew up that a red rose should have a strong rich fragrance — something that is sadly no longer always true today. Height 4ft. A hybrid between 'Gloire des Rosomanes' and 'Géant des Batailles'. Bred by Roussel (France), 1853.

BARONNE PRÉVOST, *Hybrid Perpetual.*

MRS. JOHN LAING, *Hybrid Perpetual.*

100

REINE DES VIOLETTES, *Hybrid Perpetual Rose. The best of the repeat-flowering purple Old Roses.*

GEORG ARENDS ('Fortune Besson'). The breeding of this rose was 'Frau Karl Druschki' x 'La France' and it should, therefore, technically be placed with the Hybrid Teas. In practice it conforms to neither of these classes, forming as it does a fine shapely, slightly arching shrub of 5ft. in height with plentiful foliage. The flowers, on the other hand, are of distinctly Hybrid Tea persuasion, with large high-centred buds, the petals rolling back at the edges in the most attractive manner. Its colour is a clear rose-pink and it has a delicious fragrance. It is interesting to note that even a Hybrid Tea flower can be displayed to greater advantage on taller more shrubby growth. Raised by W. Hinner (Germany), 1910.

GLOIRE DE DUCHER. No other Hybrid Perpetual can match this variety for the splendour and richness of its flowers. They form very large informal cups of a deep purple-crimson shaded with maroon and are very fragrant. The blooms are particularly fine in the cool of the autumn. The growth is strong and rather sprawly, up to 7ft. in height, with large dark green leaves, and it might well be grown on a pillar or some other form of support. Its only drawback is a susceptibility to mildew. The breeding is not known. Bred by Ducher (France), introduced 1865. See page 104.

HENRY NEVARD. The most recent variety on my list, this rose was bred by Cant's of Colchester as late as 1924 and may have some Hybrid Tea in its make up. Its large deep crimson flowers are of cupped formation, with a powerful fragrance. They are held on long stems and repeat well. It has the tall upright habit of growth of a Hybrid Perpetual, perhaps 5ft. in height. The leaves are large, leathery and deep green.

HUGH DICKSON. Introduced in 1905, this was one of the most popular roses of its day, but in spite of this it does not have very much to recommend it. The flowers are large, scarlet-crimson, of a globular formation and produced on long shoots. They tend to lack character, being unshapely and rather coarse. The growth is very tall and ungainly, 7ft., and it is perhaps more effective as a Climber when it will easily achieve 10ft. In its heyday it was frequently grown by pegging the long growth to the soil, so that it became effectively a climbing rose trailing along the ground. In this way numerous flower shoots are sent up along the stems, thus rendering it more suitable for bedding and providing an attractive 'Edwardian' effect. It flowers freely and recurrently and has a strong fragrance. The result of a cross between 'Lord Bacon' and 'Gruss an Teplitz', it was bred by H. Dickson.

JOHN HOPPER. Large fragrant lilac-pink flowers, deepening towards the centre. Vigorous, upright growth of 4ft. 'Jules Margottin' x 'Madame Vidot'. Bred by Ward (U.K.), 1862.

MABEL MORRISON. A white sport of 'Baroness Rothschild', see above, with the same Portland Rose characteristics and fine, shapely, shallowly-cupped blooms. In autumn these will sometimes take on delicate blush tints. Very little scent. Discovered by Broughton (U.K.), introduced 1878.

MRS. JOHN LAING. Bred by Henry Bennett, this may be regarded as his finest production. The flowers are large, deeply cupped, fully double and of a silvery-pink colouring. The growth is vigorous and upright, up to 4ft. in height, with greyish-green foliage. 'Mrs. John Laing' is a good reliable rose, truly recurrent flowering and strongly scented. Introduced in 1887, and one of the most popular roses of its time, it was said that Bennett received $45,000 for the distribution rights in America, an unheard of sum in those days. It was a seedling from 'François Michelon'. See page 100.

PAUL NEYRON. In the past this rose was regarded as having the largest flowers of all roses, and I suspect this may not be far from true today. It is in every way a large shrub, with large leaves and strong upright growth. Unfortunately with size comes clumsiness, as is so often the case, but if the flowers are cut and mixed with an arrangement of other flowers they can be very effective. Their colour is deep rose-pink flushed with lilac; they are cupped in shape and have a light fragrance. A cross between 'Victor Verdier' and 'Anna de Diesbach'. Bred and introduced by A. Levet (France), 1869. See page 104.

PRIDE OF WALTHAM. Large, open, thick-petalled blooms that might appear coarse were it not for its delicate pink colouring. It forms a strong plant that repeats well, but there is a possibility of mildew. Light fragrance. Height 4ft. A sport from 'Comtesse d'Oxford'. Discovered at the nursery of W. Paul & Son (U.K.), 1881.

PRINCE CAMILLE DE ROHAN ('La Rosière'). This variety has long held the reputation of being the darkest of all roses, and for this reason it continues to be in demand. I often fear that our customers may sometimes be disappointed, as it is of very weak growth, except when well grown under favourable conditions. It will form a bushy plant of 3ft., bearing medium-sized very double flowers of the richest velvety crimson-maroon. These are carried on weak stems but have a powerful fragrance. Raised by R. Verdier (France), 1861.

PAUL NEYRON, *Hybrid
Perpetual.*

SOUVENIR DU DOCTEUR JAMAIN, *Hybrid
Perpetual.*

FISHER HOLMES, *Hybrid
Perpetual.*

GLOIRE DE DUCHER, *Hybrid Perpetual.*

FERDINAND PICHARD, a striped Hybrid Perpetual Rose. The best of the repeat-flowering striped roses for the small garden.

REINE DES VIOLETTES ('Queen of the Violets'). A unique and charming rose with flowers closer to the Gallica Rose than to a typical Hybrid Perpetual. These are of full-petalled rosette formation, opening flat and quartered, with a button eye at the centre. Their colour is a deep velvet purple, turning with time to soft parma-violet. The growth is upright, about 4 or 5ft. in height, with grey-green foliage and hardly any thorns. It is reliably repeat flowering which, combined with the Old Rose form of flower, makes it particularly valuable. This rose requires good cultivation if it is to give of its best. A seedling from 'Pius IX'. Bred by Millet-Malet (France), introduced 1860. See page 101.

ROGER LAMBELIN. A sport from 'Prince Camille de Rohan', see above, with all the failings of that rose, having very weak growth and poor flowers in all but the best of conditions. In appearance, too, it is similar to 'Prince Camille de Rohan', except for the fact that its deep crimson petals are prettily edged with white. Like its parent it can be beautiful if well grown, but for most gardens it might be better to grow 'Baron Girod de l'Ain' which is much stronger. Very fragrant. Height 3ft. Discovered by Schwartz (France), distributed 1890.

SOUVENIR DU DOCTEUR JAMAIN. Not a typical Hybrid Perpetual, this rose is notable for its deep rich dark crimson colouring and its equally deep and rich perfume. The flowers are of medium size, shallow, showing just a hint of their yellow stamens. It is repeat flowering but, like so many crimson roses, does not make ideal growth, being rather lean and lanky, and about 5 or 6ft. in height. However, since there are few shrub roses with flowers of such colouring it is worth its place in the garden. It has for some years also been on sale under the name of 'Souvenir d'Alphonse Lavallée', though it is impossible to see any difference between the two roses. Introduced by Lacharme (France), 1865. See page 104.

TRIOMPHE DE L'EXPOSITION. Full-petalled cherry-red flowers, opening almost flat and quartered, with a button eye. The growth is strong and bushy with recurrent blooms. Height 5ft. Margottin (France), 1855.

ULRICH BRUNNER. A tall, robust and durable shrub of narrow, ungainly and upright habit, about 6ft. in height. The flowers are cupped in form and of a rather crude pale crimson colour. Fine blooms are sometimes produced and it is a useful rose for cutting. Strong fragrance, recurrent flowering. It creates a spectacular display at Sissinghurst Castle, where its long shoots are pegged down. Bred by Levet (France), 1881.

VICK'S CAPRICE. Very large full-cupped flowers, their colouring of deep pink lightly striped with paler pink and white providing a delicate effect. It is very fragrant, recurrent flowering, with ample foliage that comes all the way up to the flower. Height 4ft. A sport from the pure pink 'Archiduchesse Élisabeth d'Autriche' (to which it frequently reverts) found in the garden of a Mr. Vick of Rochester, New York, introduced 1891.

Tea Roses

The Tea Roses were the result of crossing two of the original China Roses, 'Hume's Blush China' and 'Parks' Yellow Tea Scented China', with various Bourbon and Noisette Roses. The first Tea Rose was introduced in 1835 and most appropriately named 'Adam', having been bred by an English nurseryman of that name. The class was originally known as Tea Scented China Roses, but this was soon abbreviated to Tea Roses. How they came to be known by this name is a mystery; there is, in fact, a range of fragrances to be found amongst them, but none of them, to my nose at least, has much in common with that of tea, although Graham Thomas insists that the scent of a typical Tea Rose is exactly like that of a freshly opened packet of China tea. However this may be, we still refer to certain roses as having a Tea Rose scent, and the name has now acquired a meaning of its own.

The Tea Rose was destined to become one of the parents of the Hybrid Tea, and could perhaps be best described as a rather slender version of that class while at the same time exhibiting a fairly close affinity to the twiggy, branching growth of the China Rose. Like the Chinas they are diploids. The popular, rather romanticised impression of a Tea Rose is of a long, slender and refined bud of the most delicate colouring, but this is only partly true; in fact they come in various forms and sometimes in quite harsh colours.

These roses cannot be recommended for general garden use, indeed I am not entirely sure that they should even be included in this book were it not for the fact that they complete the historical picture. I have grown a number of them in my garden but have never found them satisfactory in our climate. If they survive the winter they are frequently cut back by frost, and although some of them are hardier than others, they often have the appearance of rather run down Hybrid Teas. When grown in the warmer parts of the British Isles, such as

LADY HILLINGDON, *a Tea Rose with fine dark green foliage.*

Cornwall or Devon, it might be quite a different matter, and I have seen them growing as fine large shrubs in Mediterranean countries. If space can be found for them in a cold greenhouse you may expect some very beautiful roses and the connoisseur may feel this worth while; after all, is it not true that many alpine plant enthusiasts go to equal lengths to grow their own particular treasures? Another less extreme method is to plant them against a warm and sheltered wall and treat them as short Climbers.

However, it would be very worth while planting them in countries with warm and frost-free climates — most of the survivors in this class have, in fact, come from such countries. The Climbing Teas are usually much hardier and can be recommended for the average garden. Whether this is due to different breeding or to the fact that they are usually grown on walls, I cannot say — perhaps it is a bit of both. These are described in the chapter on Climbing Roses in the companion volume to this book.

CATHERINE MERMET, *Tea Rose. Representative of one of the two main classes of the late Victorian period.*

Tea Roses prefer a well-drained, fertile soil and, as the reader will have gathered, should be planted in a warm and sheltered position. Like their parents the China Roses, they object to too much pruning. This should consist only of the thinning out of old growth, the removal of dead wood, and general maintenance of the shape of the bush. Height will vary enormously according to climate. They seldom achieve more than 3ft. in the United Kingdom, but I have no doubt that in more southerly countries they could form much larger bushes.

Included here is a short list of Tea Roses that are still obtainable. As I have not grown many of them under garden conditions I have not had sufficient experience of some of the varieties to say which are the best. I have included mainly those with flowers in softer shades as I think these are more appealing.

ANNA OLIVER. Flesh-pink pointed blooms with the reverse side of the petals deep pink. Quite vigorous and bushy for a Tea Rose. Fragrant. Bred by Ducher (France), 1872.

ARCHIDUC JOSEPH. One of the most hardy of the Tea Roses, forming a strong bush or Climber, with plentiful dark green foliage. The flowers are of a purplish-pink, opening flat with many petals, gradually turning to blush at the centre. A seedling from 'Madame Lombard'. Bred by Nabonnand (France), 1872.

CATHERINE MERMET. This beautiful Tea Rose was once widely grown for the cut-flower trade. When well grown it has exquisitely formed buds which are blush-pink at the centre and tinted with lilac-pink at the edges. Only suitable for the greenhouse in the U.K. Bred by Guillot Fils (France), 1869. See page 109.

DR. GRILL. Pointed rose-pink buds shaded with copper, opening flat and full petalled. Branching growth. Fragrant. 'Ophirie' x 'Souvenir de Victor Hugo'. Bonnaire (France), 1886.

DUCHESSE DE BRABANT. Large full-petalled cupped blooms varying from soft rosy-pink to bright rose-pink. This variety is hardier than many of the others and has strong branching growth with good foliage. Very fragrant. Bernède (France), 1857.

HOMÈRE. Nicely cupped soft pink flowers with red tints at the edges, paling almost to white at the centre. An early variety that is hardier than most. It has bushy, twiggy growth with dark green foliage. Bred by Robert et Moreau (France), 1858.

LADY HILLINGDON. The only bush Tea Rose that can be said to be in anything like general circulation, and virtually as hardy as a Hybrid Tea. The recorded parentage is 'Papa Gontier' x 'Madame Hoste', both of which are Tea Roses, but this is doubtful due to the fact that the chromosome count indicates a cross with a Hybrid Tea. This illustrates very well that we should not place too much credence on early breeding records. 'Lady Hillingdon' has large petals, forming long slender buds of a lovely deep apricot-yellow which eventually open to rather shapeless flowers with a strong Tea Rose fragrance. It has fine contrasting dark green foliage which is coppery-mahogany when young. There is a particularly good climbing sport, better by far than the bush, and it is wiser to grow it in this form wherever space is available; see the chapter on Climbing Roses in the companion volume to this book. Bred by Lowe & Shawyer (U.K.), 1910. See page 108.

LADY PLYMOUTH. Large well-formed pointed buds of ivory-cream faintly flushed with pink. Bushy growth, with rather sparse dark green foliage. Slightly scented. A. Dickson (U.K.), 1914.

MADAME BRAVY ('Adele Pradel', 'Madame de Sertat'). Large creamy-white flowers shaded buff, with a strong Tea Rose fragrance. Guillot Père (France), 1846.

MADAME DE TARTAS. Large, full blush-pink flowers of cupped formation. Fairly vigorous with spreading growth and good frost resistance. A very important rose in the development of the Hybrid Teas, but there is some doubt as to whether the rose now in circulation is the correct one. Fragrant. Bernède (France), 1859.

MAMAN COCHET. Large globular blooms of pale pink, deepening towards the centre with lemon-yellow shades at the base. The growth is quite vigorous with dark green foliage. Once a famous exhibition rose. 'Marie van Houtte' x 'Madame Lombard'. Bred by Cochet (France), 1893.

MARIE VAN HOUTTE. Large pointed buds of cream tinged carmine-pink, with buff at the base of the petals. Fragrant. Sprawling habit. 'Madame de Tartas' x 'Madame Falcot'. Ducher (France), 1871.

PAPA GONTIER. Long, pointed, deep pink buds, with the reverse side of the petals carmine-red, opening semi-double. Bushy growth. Nabonnand (France), 1883.

PERLE DES JARDINS. Pointed buds developing into fragrant full-petalled flowers of a straw-yellow colour. These fail to open well in damp weather. The growth is slender but reasonably hardy. Fragrant. 'Madame Falcot' x a seedling. Levet (France), 1874.

ROSETTE DELIZY. Pointed buds of apricot and yellow, the reverse of the petals being tinted with carmine. 'Général Gallieni' x 'Comtesse Bardi'. Nabonnand (France), 1922.

SAFRANO. Pretty pointed buds of saffron-yellow and apricot, opening to semi-double flowers paling with age. Beauregard (France), 1839.

THE BRIDE. A white sport of 'Catherine Mermet', see above, and similar in every way except colour. Only for the greenhouse. Discovered by May (U.S.A.), 1885.

TRIOMPHE DU LUXEMBOURG. Full-petalled flowers borne in clusters. Salmon-pink becoming salmon-buff. Hardy (France), 1839.

WILLIAM R. SMITH ('Charles Dingee', 'Blush Maman Cochet', 'President William Smith', 'Jeanette Heller'). Shapely pointed buds; pale-pink at the centre, with the outer petals creamy-blush tinted with yellow at the base. Bred by Bagg (U.S.A.), introduced 1908.

LADY CURZON, *a Rosa rugosa hybrid with large silky-textured flowers on a sprawling shrub.*

BELLE POITEVINE, *a shapely Rugosa Rose with large flowers.*

CHAPTER 4

Rugosa Roses

R osa rugosa is a native of northern China, Japan and Korea. It was grown as a garden shrub in China, where it was said to have been used for pot-pourri, and Bunyard in his book *Old Garden Roses* (1936) speaks of a drawing by Chao Ch'ang who lived about A.D. 1000. It was also grown in Japan, and this explains why its descendants are sometimes known as Japanese Roses. The exact date of its arrival in Britain seems to be in some doubt, but it is thought to have been first introduced by the nurserymen Lee and Kennedy of Hammersmith in 1796. It forms a vigorous and sturdy shrub of up to 8ft. in height and as much across. It has very numerous strong thorns and rough-textured apple-green leaves. The flowers are large, 3½ to 4ins. across, of a variable purple-rose colouring, and have a light fragrance. These are followed by giant red tomato-shaped hips of 1in. or more in diameter. The stamens are creamy rather than the usual yellow, and this assorts well with the flower colour. It has two other important qualities: first, it is extremely hardy, and secondly it is almost alone among wild roses in its ability to repeat its flowering throughout the summer, so much so that later in the season the ripe hips can be seen on the branch at the same time as the last blooms. Although the colouring of the flowers may not be to everyone's taste, it is, in fact, a very fine shrub that can be relied upon to thrive in the poorest sandy soils.

With all these virtues, it is not surprising that a large number of hybrids have been raised and that these have become recognised as a class in their own right. Most of them were bred in the period immediately before and after the turn of the century when some excellent shrubs were produced combining the shrubby virtues of *R. rugosa* with the varying colours of the garden roses of the time. These hybrids are also large shrubs, and many of them have inherited the recurrent-flowering character of the species. Often they have lost some of the grace and bushiness of this parent, and some do not have its fine hips, but they form an often beautiful and very useful class. In spite of this, one cannot help feeling this group has never reached its full potential; after the first flush of interest little work has been done on them. This is perhaps largely due to the fact that the wrong parents have been used. *R. rugosa* is a diploid, while most garden roses are tetraploid and this has resulted in sterile offsprings, thus blocking further progress. However, such problems can be overcome, and a rich field of endeavour is open to future breeders. I feel sure that the Rugosas have it in them to be the best of all large garden shrub roses, so many of the required virtues are already inherent in the species.

The Rugosas are far removed from the roses of the West in their overall appearance. Indeed, they seem to have an almost Oriental character, both in flower and growth, and would look quite in place in a Chinese painting. One less fortunate result of this is that they do not always make a happy marriage when hybridized with garden roses. When the hybrid leans towards the Rugosa side of the parentage, all is well, but when it leans towards the other parent, the result can sometimes be rather clumsy. The variety 'Ruskin' is an example of this problem. In fact, these roses are rather unusual in that they seem to lean quite distinctly either towards their Rugosa parent on the one hand, or towards the garden rose on the other, seldom anywhere in between, and I shall try to make clear to which type they belong in each of the descriptions. It is necessary to take this factor into account when trying to visualise them in position in the garden.

Rugosa Hybrids are easily grown and require the minimum of attention. Pruning can be restricted to the thinning and removal of old and weak wood, also — and more importantly — to the encouragement of a shapely shrub, particularly with those varieties that tend towards a gaunt and rather upright growth.

Rugosas form excellent and impenetrable hedges or barriers, they are ideal for poor soil where other roses might find it difficult to thrive, and they are useful for seaside planting, withstanding the buffeting of the wind better than most roses. I have seen them growing quite happily on sand dunes — an ability they share only with the Scotch Roses, at least in so far as garden roses are concerned.

AGNES. This is a cross between *Rosa rugosa* and *R. foetida* 'Persiana', and the latter parent has placed a strong stamp upon it. The result is a rose that is still very much a Rugosa but with typically Old Rose flowers and many small petals of yellow tinted with amber, later fading to cream. It is, in effect, a yellow Old Rose, and this gives it a particular value to those in favour of this form. A mixture of the not altogether pleasing scent of *R. foetida* 'Persiana', and the scent of the Rugosa, has resulted in a delicate and unusual fragrance in this rose. The growth is upright, bushy and strong, perhaps 7ft. in height and 5ft. across, with rather small, pale green leaves. It is subject to rust in some gardens. Bred by B. & W. Saunders (Canada), introduced 1922. See page 117.

BELLE POITEVINE. A shapely shrub of 5ft. in height by as much across, and close to *Rosa rugosa* in its general appearance, having large semi-double, loosely-formed flowers of mallow-pink that open flat to show creamy-white stamens. They have a slight fragrance and are followed by large orange-red hips. Raised by G. Bruant (France), introduced 1894. See page 113.

BLANC DOUBLE DE COUBERT. A rose with all the appearance of a double form of *Rosa rugosa* 'Alba'. The flowers are large, pure white, sometimes tinged with blush in the bud, the petals having an almost papery appearance and opening semi-double with a strong fragrance. The growth is very similar to *R. rugosa* 'Alba', but a little less strong. The breeder, Cochet-Cochet of France, claimed that it was the result of a cross between *R. rugosa* and the beautiful Tea Rose 'Sombreuil'. It would be easy to come to the conclusion that there has been some mistake here, not an uncommon occurrence among older roses. However, *R. rugosa* is so dominant a seed parent that it frequently leaves little trace of the pollen parent, and it is quite possible the parentage is as the breeder stated. This is one of the best of the Rugosas, growing well and flowering with remarkable continuity. There are only a few hips. Height 5ft. 1892. See page 116.

Three Rugosa Roses.
Above: NYVELDT'S WHITE.
Above right: BLANC DOUBLE DE COUBERT.
Right: SCHNEEZWERG.

CARMEN. A variety with small and, individually, quite attractive single, dark crimson flowers. Unfortunately the growth is rather upright and the flowers do not show up well, the whole effect being one of imbalance and poverty. It was a cross between *Rosa rugosa rosea* and the Hybrid Perpetual 'Princesse de Béarn'. Bred by Lambert (Germany), 1907.

CONRAD FERDINAND MEYER (more conveniently known as 'Conrad F. Meyer'). The parentage of this rose is 'Gloire de Dijon' x 'Duc de Rohan'

AGNES, *a Rugosa Rose with a delicate fragrance.*

x a form of *Rosa rugosa*. Its growth is very tall and upright, with unusually long strong stems shooting freely from the base, so that it can, if desired, be grown as a Climber. There are numerous strong thorns, and the foliage is about half-way between that of a Hybrid Tea and *R. rugosa*. This rose has always been available in nursery catalogues, even at the time when Shrub Roses were almost entirely neglected. The reason lies, perhaps, in its large Hybrid Tea-like blooms. These are of a soft silvery-pink with the petals nicely rolled at the edges. Later they open into large, cupped, informal flowers. The fragrance is, to me, one of the most delicious of any to be found among roses, and very strong. It is interesting to note that *R. rugosa* has only a light scent, but when crossed with other roses it often produces seedlings with a very strong scent. This rose is best pruned to half its height in order to form a reasonably shapely shrub, and if it is not to exhibit its flowers to the sky only. It flowers freely and produces a good second crop later in the summer. The height will depend on pruning, but left to its own devices it will easily reach 10ft. Bred by Müller (Germany), introduced 1899.

DELICATA. A rather weak shrub by Rugosa standards, growing to little more than 3ft. in height, and it would, therefore, not be a first choice except where space is limited. It is otherwise close to *Rosa rugosa* in general appearance. The flowers are semi-double and of a pleasing soft lilac-pink. Raised by Cooling (U.S.A), introduced 1898.

DR. ECKENER. One of the most massive and powerful of the Rugosas; so much so that few can find space for it, and severe pruning leads only to more growth and less flowers. It may have its uses in poor soils. The blooms are coppery-yellow, becoming pink and yellow with age, and are large and of Hybrid Tea character. Excessively thorny. A coarse rose though it has a strong fragrance. Height 10ft. The breeding is 'Golden Emblem' x a *Rosa rugosa* hybrid. Bred by Berger (Germany), introduced 1931.

FIMBRIATA ('Phoebe's Frilled Pink', 'Dianthiflora'). This pretty rose has, as its various names indicate, flowers fringed at the edges in the manner of a pink. This is probably the result of some breakdown in the genetic make up of the plant, due to the difficult step between its two widely separated parents, *Rosa rugosa* and the vigorous Noisette Rose 'Madame Alfred Carrière'. Such peculiarities do occur in many garden plants in the course of hybridization — in this case the result is a happy one. In spite of the robust nature of both parents 'Fimbriata' is not a particularly vigorous shrub, although adequately so. The growth is rather slim with quite small, light green foliage. The flowers are small, soft pink, fragrant and held in clusters. It has a delicacy that is more beautiful than we find in its more robust competitors the Grootendorst Roses. Height 4ft. Bred by Morlet (France), 1891. See page 120.

F.J. GROOTENDORST. Like 'Fimbriata' this variety has small flowers with fringed petals, but in this case the results are less pleasing. It is a cross between *Rosa rugosa* 'Rubra' and the Polyantha Pompon Rose 'Madame Norbert Levavasseur'. The flowers, which are of a rather dull crimson, lack the delicacy of 'Fimbriata' and are carried rather too tightly in their sprays. The growth is very strong, upright and bushy, and the leaves show signs of its Polyantha parentage. It has no scent. On the plus side it is strong and entirely reliable and flowers more repeatedly than any other of the Rugosas, except its own sport and the species itself. It has in fact three sports: 'Pink Grootendorst', 'Grootendorst Supreme' and 'White Grootendorst', all of which are of very similar character and detailed below. Height 5ft. Raised by de Goey (Holland), introduced 1918.

FRU DAGMAR HASTRUP ('Frau Dagmar Hartopp'). A widely planted rose and a favourite with municipal authorities, no doubt because it lends itself to mass planting, being of short, bushy growth which can be pruned fairly hard without losing bloom. It might best be described as a shorter, light pink form of *Rosa rugosa*. The flowers are beautiful and delicate in appearance, the buds long and pointed and of a rich pink, opening to a clear light pink with creamy-white stamens. They are produced repeatedly and are followed by large deep red hips. Fragrant. It is thought to be a seedling from *R. rugosa*. Height 4ft. Hastrup (Denmark), 1914. See page 120.

GROOTENDORST SUPREME. A sport from 'F.J. Grootendorst', see above, with darker, garnet-red flowers. It is said to be rather less vigorous than its parent, to which, except for colour, it is similar. Yellowish-green leaves. Slight fragrance. 4ft. Grootendorst (Holland), 1936.

HANSA. At first sight this variety seems to be very similar to 'Roseraie de l'Hay', but on closer observation it soon becomes clear that it is a less beautiful rose. The flowers are fully double and of deep crimson-purple. It is strong, hardy and healthy, and from a nurseryman's point of view has the advantage that it propagates much more easily than 'Roseraie de l'Hay'. Typical Rugosa type. Fragrant. Height 4ft. Introduced by Schaum & Van Tol (Holland), 1905.

LADY CURZON. The parentage of this rose is *Rosa* 'Macrantha' x *R. rugosa* 'Rubra', a very promising cross and the result does not disappoint us. It forms a tangled shrub of some 8ft. in height and the same in width. The leaves are rough textured, like those of its Rugosa parent, and there are many strong thorns. The flowers are large, single and about 4ins. across, of a light iridescent pink, paling almost to white at the centre, with petals like crumpled silk and a fine boss of golden stamens. They are fragrant but not recurrent. This variety is excellent in the border or in the more wild areas of the garden, where it will scramble quite happily for 20ft. in all directions in shrubs and trees if required, providing charming natural effects. Raised by Turner (U.K.), introduced 1901. See page 112.

MADAME GEORGES BRUANT. A cross between *Rosa rugosa* and the beautiful Tea Rose 'Sombreuil', resulting in a tall, narrow and somewhat ungainly shrub. The flowers start as shapely pointed buds of creamy-white and open to pure white flowers with three or four rows of petals and yellow stamens. They are held in small clusters which appear both in summer and autumn. Fragrant. Height 5ft. Raised by Bruant (France), introduced 1887.

FRU DAGMAR HASTRUP, *a popular Rugosa Rose with delicate flowers.*

FIMBRIATA, *a Rugosa Rose with fringed petals like a pink.*

PINK GROOTENDORST, *another fringed Rugosa Rose, stronger and less dainty than 'Fimbriata'.*

Opposite: MAX GRAF, *a Rosa rugosa hybrid and one of the best of the ground-cover roses.*

SARAH VAN FLEET, *one of the most reliable Rugosa hybrids.*

MAX GRAF. A trailing rose and one of the best varieties for ground cover. The result of a cross between *Rosa rugosa* and *R. wichuraiana,* gaining its prostrate habit from the latter. It forms a thicket of growth about 2ft. deep and spreads over a wide area, its long shoots sometimes rooting themselves into the ground as they go. The flowers are of small to medium size, single, pale pink to almost white at the centre, with

yellow stamens, and have the fresh, fruit-like fragrance of their Wichuraiana parent. It has plentiful, dark, glossy foliage, and flowers only in the early summer. A useful rose, not only in the border, but also for covering banks and other problem areas where dense ground cover is required. Bred by Bowditch (U.S.A.), 1919.

MICRUGOSA. See the chapter on Species Roses in the companion to this volume.

MICRUGOSA ALBA. See the chapter on Species Roses in the companion to this volume.

MRS. ANTHONY WATERER. Of all the Rugosas that are of obvious hybrid appearance, this is in many ways the most satisfactory. It has excellent leafy growth of 5ft. in height, spreading broadly to form a dense and shapely, domed shrub. Both flower and foliage are close to that of an Old Rose. The blooms open wide, full and slightly cupped and are of crimson colouring, with a strong fragrance. It produces an unfailingly good crop of flowers in early summer, followed by only occasional blooms later. If it was also repeat flowering this rose would be hard to beat. The parents were the Hybrid Perpetual 'Général Jaqueminot' x unnamed Rugosa hybrid. Introduced by Waterer (U.K.), 1898. See page 124.

NOVA ZEMBLA. A colour sport of 'Conrad Ferdinand Meyer', see above, the flowers being white with the very slightest tinge of pink. Equally good and similar in every way to its parent, although perhaps a little less vigorous. Discovered by Mees (U.K.), 1907.

NYVELDT'S WHITE. A beautiful single white rose, which might at first sight easily be mistaken for the excellent *Rosa rugosa* 'Alba'; closer observation reveals a rose of more refined appearance and rather more graceful growth. The leaves are smoother and their leaflets narrower and of a paler green than those of 'Alba'. The flowers are more elongated in the petal and about 4ins. across. They are fragrant, repeat well, and are followed by plentiful large, orange-red hips. A very good shrub. The parentage is stated as being (*R. rugosa* 'Rubra' x *R. cinnamomea*) x *R. nitida*. This is a little surprising, as there are no white roses in this cross, and it may be that *R. rugosa* 'Alba' was used rather than *R. rugosa* 'Rubra'. Raised by Nyveldt (Holland), introduced 1955. See page 116.

PAULII. See the chapter on Species Roses in the companion to this volume.

PAULII ROSEA. See the chapter on Species Roses in the companion to this volume.

PINK GROOTENDORST. A pink sport of 'F.J. Grootendorst', see above. Like its parent it is vigorous, though perhaps a little less so than the original, forming a strong, bushy, reliably repeat-flowering shrub. Discovered by Grootendorst (Holland), 1923. See page 120.

ROBUSTA. A recent introduction from Kordes of Germany. It bears abundant medium-sized, single, bright scarlet-red flowers continuously throughout the summer. The growth is very strong and dense, with many thorns and ample leathery, dark green foliage. There is a slight fragrance. This promises to be a useful addition to the Rugosas. The breeding was unnamed seedling x *Rosa rugosa* 'Regeliana'. Introduced 1979.

ROSA RUGOSA ALBA. An almost faultless if little sung shrub of good vigorous growth, 6ft. high by as much across, with ample foliage. It bears large 4in. pure white flowers which open from long, slender buds throughout the summer. These are followed by very large tomato-like orange-red hips that ripen together with the last of its blooms. Slight fragrance. This rose was originally a sport from *Rosa rugosa typica,* and as such would not come from true seed. However, strains have been developed that are almost pure, although the occasional purple-flowered plant will still occur. Seedling bushes of both *R. rugosa* 'Alba' and *R. rugosa typica* are ideal for massed landscape planting, particularly in public places, as both flower continuously throughout the summer, spreading and suckering freely to form a continuous thicket and, most importantly in such planting, they do not have the problem of suckering from a stock (anyone involved in landscape designing and maintenance will be well aware of the problems presented by suckers in the middle of a hundred closely planted 6ft. tall thorny shrub roses!). See page 125.

ROSA RUGOSA RUBRA (*R. rugosa* 'Atropurpurea'). A selected form from the species *R. rugosa typica.* The flowers are of a richer crimson, with the usual contrasting creamy stamens. It is a considerable improvement on the original. See page 125.

ROSA RUGOSA TYPICA (*R. rugosa rugosa*). This is a form of *R. rugosa* described in the introduction to this group. It is considered typical of the species, although it cannot be depended on to reproduce itself exactly from seed. *R. rugosa* is, in fact, a very variable species.

MRS. ANTHONY WATERER, *a Rugosa Rose producing a good crop of flowers with a strong fragrance.*

ROSERAIE DE L'HAY. A vigorous shrub, perhaps 8ft. in height, with fine dense spreading growth and luxurious typically Rugosa foliage. The flowers are very large and double, opening wide from attractively pointed buds, their colour a rich crimson-purple with a few creamy stamens to be seen among the petals. They are studded evenly among its leafy growth, showing themselves to perfection. It is one of the most beautiful and completely reliable shrub roses, repeating well, but with

SCABROSA, *a strong, bushy Rugosa Rose.*

ROSA RUGOSA ALBA, *an almost faultless Rugosa Rose.*

ROSA RUGOSA RUBRA. *Note how it is producing hips at the same time as flowers.*

ROSERAIE DE L'HAY, *one of the best of the Rugosa Roses.*

very few hips. Similar to 'Hansa', see above, but finer and of richer colouring. Said to be a double sport from *Rosa rugosa,* but this is doubtful. Bred by Cochet-Cochet (France), 1901, and named after the magnificent rose garden near Paris.

RUSKIN. A cross between the Rugosa 'Souvenir de Pierre Leperdrieux' and 'Victor Hugo', it is the latter rose, a typical red Hybrid Perpetual, which has proved to be the dominant parent, with not altogether good results. It is true that it produces large and sumptuous rich scarlet-crimson cupped flowers of Old Rose character, but these are often misshapen and clumsy. Moreover, the growth is very tall and narrow, and by no means satisfactory. This can be improved by cutting the rose down to half its height each year, or it may be trained as a Climbing Rose. It has a rich and pleasing fragrance, but there is little or no repeat flowering. Height anything up to 8ft. Raised by Van Fleet (U.S.A.), introduced 1928.

SARAH VAN FLEET. A strong, bushy, upright shrub of 7ft. in height and 5ft. across. It is one of the most useful and reliable of the Rugosa hybrids, both for garden and municipal planting, especially at the backs of borders. The flowers are large, semi-double, opening wide and slightly cupped, china pink in colour, with yellow stamens. They are usually held in small clusters and appear both in summer and autumn. The growth and foliage is typically Rugosa, with rough-textured leaves and many thorns. Bred by Dr. Van Fleet of the U.S.A., reputedly from a cross between *Rosa rugosa* and 'My Maryland', but a chromosome count seems to place some doubt upon this. Introduced 1926. See page 121.

SCABROSA. Whether or not this is a selection from *Rosa rugosa* or a hybrid is hard to say. Certainly it has everything in common with the species, except that it is of more substance in every way. The flowers are very large, single and about 5½ ins. across. Their colour is a rich violet-crimson with pale contrasting stamens. The growth is strong, spreading and bushy, with large, thick, very rugose leaves and many thorns. It has a slight fragrance and bears massive hips. Height 4 or 5ft. It was first introduced by Harkness & Co., of Hitchin, but Jack Harkness of that firm, in his book *Roses,* takes no credit for its breeding, saying it was discovered amongst a batch of a rose called 'Rose Apples', but otherwise being unable to say anything of its origin. See page 124.

SCHNEELICHT. There have been a number of successful hybrids between *Rosa rugosa* and other wild species, and this is one of them, being the result of a cross with *R. phoenicea*. It forms a broad mound of growth about 5ft. in height and 8ft. across, sending up long, arching branches that bear clusters of flowers all along their length. These start as pointed blush-tinted buds, opening to pure white single flowers of medium size with yellow stamens. It has dark green foliage close to that of *R. rugosa*. A useful ground-cover rose. Bred by Geschwind (Hungary), introduced 1894.

SCHNEEZWERG ('Snowdwarf'). Reputedly a hybrid of *Rosa bracteata*, and from this species it may have inherited its dark, shiny foliage which bears little resemblance to a Rugosa. Its outstanding virtues are its compact, twiggy growth and shapely habit, together with its ability to flower continuously throughout the summer. The flowers are quite small, semi-double and purest white, with pale yellow stamens. They repeat well and are followed by pretty, small, orange-red hips. Height about 5ft. A good and reliable shrub, if a little unexciting. Raised by P. Lambert (Germany), introduced 1912. See page 116.

SOUVENIR DE PHILEMON COCHET. A sport from 'Blanc Double de Coubert', with very much more double flowers. These might be described as being similar to those of a double hollyhock, with large, rather papery outer petals enclosing numerous small inner petals. At their best they are very beautiful and quite unique, but unfortunately rather subject to damage in damp weather, and it would perhaps be better to avoid this rose in particularly moist areas. It forms a rather smaller shrub than its parent, but otherwise the growth is the same. 5ft. Discovered by Cochet-Cochet (France), 1899.

VANGUARD. An excessively vigorous and rather coarse shrub with large glossy foliage and large ill-formed flowers of modern appearance, orange-salmon in colour. It does not flower very freely, and if pruned continues to make more growth at the expense of flowers. Very fragrant. Breeding *Rosa wichuraiana* x *R. rugosa* 'Alba' x 'Eldorado'. Height up to 10ft. It can be used as a Climber. Stevens (U.S.A.), 1932.

WHITE GROOTENDORST. A white sport of 'Pink Grootendorst', the second in a line of sports from 'F.J. Grootendorst', see above, though the growth does not seem to be so strong as that of its forebears. In fact, there is often a decline in vigour when a sport occurs. Discovered by Eddy (U.S.A.), introduced 1962.

BOW BELLS, *an English Rose with pretty cupped flowers.*

CHAPTER 5
English Roses

We have followed the history of the Old Roses from earliest times through to the peak of their popularity in the 18th and 19th centuries, and I have described the many beautiful varieties that have been preserved for our pleasure in the present day. I have said how most of these roses flower only in the early summer and that it was only at the end of this period that we began to get roses that flower throughout the summer. These were the China Roses, the Portland Roses, the Bourbon Roses and the Hybrid Perpetuals. These repeat-flowering roses had but a short period of popularity, for it was not long before the Hybrid Teas which we find in most gardens today took over in popularity and almost completely wiped the Old Roses off the garden scene.

This was to my mind a tragedy, for the Old Rose flower had a charm and a beauty that was quite different to that of the Hybrid Teas. In fact, I would say they had a much greater beauty. It was also particularly unfortunate, as the repeat-flowering Old Roses – that is to say those described in Chapter 3: Old Roses II – were never really developed to their full potential. In spite of the fact that they have an undeniable beauty, they are often unreliable and subject to disease and are by no means always reliably repeat-flowering. They also have the limited colour range of their forebears. There are virtually no yellows, apricots or peach shades. Crimson tends to be lacking in all but the Hybrid Perpetuals, which were themselves quickly moving towards the Hybrid Tea in character of flower and growth. All in all, it is true to say that there are no more than a few really good repeat-flowering Old Roses.

It was with these thoughts in mind that I set out to breed a new race of roses, which I have called 'English Roses'. These are the result of crossing the Old Roses with Modern Hybrid Teas and Floribundas. They combine the unique character and beauty of the Old Roses, together with something of their natural and more graceful shrubby growth, with the excellent repeat-flowering qualities of the Modern Roses. They also combine with this all the varying colours that we find in Modern Roses. English Roses are in fact new 'Old Roses', if I may be forgiven for the apparent contradiction in terms.

In addition, the English Roses have a particularly strong fragrance, which they inherit from the old varieties. Indeed, I think it is no exaggeration to say that they are the most fragrant of all roses – not excluding the Old Roses themselves. This is perhaps because I have always been very careful to breed almost exclusively from fragrant varieties.

Their breeding began some thirty years ago, but although I had made crosses earlier than this, it was only when I hybridized the beautiful

BIBI MAIZOON, *English Rose. Superb 'Old Rose' of purest colour. Usually more distinctly cupped than this.*

BELLE STORY, *an English Rose with an attractively incurved form of flower.*

Floribunda 'Dainty Maid' (bred by E.B. Le Grice) with the charming little Gallica 'Belle Isis', to produce the now popular 'Constance Spry', that they really began to get under way. 'Constance Spry' is a large Shrub or Climbing Rose of exceptionally strong growth, bearing giant but always refined flowers of a lovely shade of glowing pink. It made a considerable stir among those who favour Old Roses, for it had all the characteristics of such roses, and this was exactly what I was looking for. 'Constance Spry' was, however, only once flowering. With this in mind I crossed it back to certain other recurrent flowering modern varieties. Among these were the Floribunda 'Ma Perkins' for its cupped, old type flowers; the Hybrid Tea 'Monique' for the purity of its pink colouring; and 'Madame Caroline Testout', a tough old Hybrid Tea with flowers of Old Rose formation.

Meanwhile, I crossed another of Le Grice's Floribundas, 'Dusky Maiden', with the deep crimson Gallica 'Tuscany' to get shades of red. This also gave me a once-flowering rose of the old type, the deep wine-crimson 'Chianti'. I again crossed this with an early Hybrid Tea called 'Château de Clos Vougeot', notable as a parent of deep crimsons which do not fade. It is also a rose of spreading habit, something which I much desired in English Roses. Unfortunately it tends to yield seedlings of rather weak growth, and it was necessary to cross its progeny with other strong-growing red varieties.

We now had two strains, a pink and a red, and these formed the basis of the breed. Since then, other roses have been brought in, always with the objective of improving the shrubby nature of the plant, while retaining and enhancing the Old Rose appearance of the flowers. Notable among these has been 'Iceberg', itself closely related to the Hybrid Musk Roses and, to my mind, one of the finest Floribundas ever bred. Its influence shows up in such varieties as 'Graham Thomas', 'Perdita' and 'Heritage'.

To gain increased vigour some Modern Climbers, such as 'Aloha' and 'Parade' have been used; both are very fragrant and vigorous and have close affinities to the Old Roses in the form of their flowers. Other roses used have been 'Louise Odier', 'Conrad Ferdinand Meyer', 'Golden Wings' and 'Chinatown' — the latter two in order to introduce yellow colouring. There were of course others, and as you read through my descriptions of the various varieties these will become clear. There were of course also many crosses that were failures.

Before going any further into my thoughts and theories on English Roses, I would like to describe all the varieties of these roses that are available at the present day. In describing these, I shall perhaps be able to give a fairly good idea of their true nature.

First of all, however, perhaps I should give a few points on cultivation as this concerns English Roses in particular. Further information of a more general nature will be found in Chapter 7.

As regards the cultivation of English Roses, there are a few points that should be borne in mind. It must be remembered that English Roses are repeat-flowering, like the Chinas, the Bourbons and Modern Roses. If we wish to be sure of flowers later in the season it is necessary to give them fertile soil and to feed them well, if possible giving them some form of natural manure. It is also essential that there should be moisture if flowering is to continue throughout the summer. Without this growth must cease, and with it flowering. Mulching is helpful and, during dry spells, watering. This is true of all recurrent-flowering roses, and particularly those of a shrubby nature.

Pruning is also more important with repeat-flowering Shrub Roses, and so it is with English Roses. It may vary depending on the gardener's own requirements, but in general it is best to prune back the growth to two-thirds or one-half of its length, having first removed weak, ageing or dead branches. This may be interpreted with some freedom: longer growth will probably result in less continuous flowering; on the other hand it may provide a more attractive shrub. Due attention should be paid to the building up of well balanced growth.

I prefer to prune in January or in late autumn, although it is more usual to recommend March. The growth of roses starts very early. If we prune late we remove shoots that are already growing well. This does not matter except for the fact that we are delaying flowering because the growth will have to start all over again, and this can sometimes mean that the second or third crop of flowers arrives so late in the season that it is caught by late frosts. All repeat-flowering Shrub Roses, and particularly English Roses, require time to generate further growth and flowers. Early pruning means that the second crop will start while there is still likely to be moisture in the soil.

The less vigorous English varieties can be pruned to within a few inches of the ground to provide bushes, and so pruned should repeat well for it is hard pruning that makes the modern bush rose so excellent in this respect. It will also render them more suitable for beds and for very small gardens. They may not, however, show themselves to such good effect and will lose something of their natural grace.

Large growers may be allowed to grow into tall shrubs, and can be planted at the back of the border. In such cases very little pruning will be given, except removing old wood and trimming out weak and dead shoots. With such pruning repeat flowering would be considerably reduced.

The soft colours of the English Roses mix admirably with those of Old and Shrub Roses, providing continuity when the latter have finished flowering. English Roses also mix well with other plants in the border but, as with all recurrent-flowering roses, cannot withstand too much competition, so it is necessary to keep them at a reasonable distance from other strong-growing plants.

Most people with small gardens will plant Shrub Roses singly. Here, this is perfectly satisfactory, but I cannot stress too strongly the advantages of planting them in close groups of two or three. In this way one plant runs into the other to provide a more bushy whole and, incidentally, assuring us of a more continuous flowering, for when one plant has temporarily ceased to flower the others may take over.

ABRAHAM DARBY, *English Rose. A shapely, medium sized shrub producing large cupped flowers with unusual freedom and continuity.*

Right: BREDON, *a short, tough English Rose flowering freely and repeatedly.*

CHARLES AUSTIN, *English Rose. Very large flowers and strong, rather upright growth.*

All repeat-flowering roses of whatever kind have an enormous task in producing so many blooms throughout the summer and will have difficulty in making a really satisfactory shrub. This is why we tend to grow Hybrid Teas closely planted in beds or borders; a Hybrid Tea standing on its own does not amount to very much. Although English Roses are stronger, the same problem arises. It is a well known fact that most plants look better planted in groups. Experienced gardeners seldom plant any plant singly, except perhaps large shrubs. The same is true of English Roses.

English Roses have been in the process of development now for a number of years, and it is inevitable that the more recent varieties are greatly superior to some of the earlier ones. Our varieties of less recent introduction are often no less beautiful, but not all of them behave so well in the garden. I have therefore decided in this edition of my book, to mark what I regard as the more reliable and outstanding of the English Roses with *. I hope this will not entirely divert gardeners and collectors from growing my other varieties, as they are still very worthwhile, particularly when given a little extra care and a favourable position.

I regard the ideas expressed in the above two paragraphs – that is to say grouping and selection of varieties – as vital, if one is to get the maximum out of English Roses.

English Roses

 * ABRAHAM DARBY. This variety is unusual among English Roses in that it is the result of a cross between two Modern Roses, the Floribunda 'Yellow Cushion', and 'Aloha' a Modern Climber, although both parents bear flowers similar to those of an Old Rose. 'Abraham Darby' is very much a Shrub Rose, forming a fine plant of up to 5ft. in height with long, arching growth, and glossy foliage. The flowers, in spite of the parentage, are of truly Old Rose formation, large, deeply cupped and loosely filled with petals. The colour is soft peachy-pink on the inside of the petals and a pale yellow on the outside. The centre petals fold and turn inwards to give a mixture of yellow and pink. All these colours fade towards the edge of the flower as it ages, providing a soft and pleasing effect. There is a strong and delicious fragrance. It is hardy, disease resistant and recurrent flowering. Austin (U.K.), 1985. See page 134.

AMBRIDGE ROSE. This is a good all-round garden rose. It flowers very freely and continuously, has neat, bushy growth, and could equally well be used for a border or for rose beds. The flowers are of medium size, nicely cupped at first, opening to a loose rosette formation; their colour is deep apricot at the centre, paling to the outer edges of the flower. Height 2½ft. Named at the request of the B.B.C. for their long-running 'Archers' serial. Breeding, 'Charles Austin' x 'Seedling'. Austin (U.K.), 1990.

BELLE STORY. The flowers of this rose are large, perfectly symmetrical in outline, with the petals opening wide and incurving towards the edges, with a fine boss of stamens at their centre; the whole giving the impression of a semi-double peony. They are held in small and medium-sized sprays. The colour is a delicate shade of pink, fading slightly towards the edge of the flower. It has a pleasant fragrance. A strong and healthy shrub of about 4ft. in height. Belle Story was one of the first nursing sisters to serve as an officer in the Royal Navy. Austin (U.K.), 1984. See page 131.

BIBI MAIZOON. I was very excited when I first saw this rose bloom, as it seemed to a large degree to represent an ideal English Rose. The growth is nicely arched, forming an elegant shrub, and the flowers, which are of medium size, are of perfect deeply cupped formation. They are filled with petals and are of the richest, purest pink imaginable. They are also very fragrant. Unfortunately, it has shown a shyness to bloom in the first year or two after planting. Breeding, 'The Reeve' x 'Chaucer'. Austin (U.K.), 1989. See page 130.

BOW BELLS. A good strong-growing, bushy shrub, but not a typical English Rose — nearer to a Floribunda. The flowers are small to medium in size, of a strong pink colouring, distinctly cup-shaped and held in large sprays, giving a charming bell-like effect. This should be a very useful rose which will grow well under any reasonable conditions. Fragrant. Some 4ft. high and perhaps 3½ft. across. Austin (U.K.) 1991. See page 128.

BREDON. Had this rose been introduced as a Floribunda it might well have made a reputation for itself on the popular market, for it has many of the qualities looked for in a Floribunda. It is a short but vigorous little bush, producing many small flowers in large sprays so that the plant is covered with bloom. The flowers, however, are much nearer the old tradition, being small, perfectly formed rosettes of about 2½ins. across and made up of numerous little petals. Their colour is a buff-yellow shade, deeper at the centre, paling towards the edge. They have

CHAUCER, *an English Rose with Old Rose flowers and a strong myrrh scent.*

CHARLES RENNIE MACKINTOSH, *English Rose. A pleasing shade of lilac (more lilac than this picture). Free wiry growth.*

BROTHER CADFAEL *is of the largest English Roses, but never lacking in* *refinement.*

a strong fruit-like Rambler Rose fragrance. It might be used as a low hedge. Height 3ft. 'Wife of Bath' x and 'Lilian Austin'. Austin (U.K.), 1984. See page 135.

* BROTHER CADFAEL. Here we have a rose with exceptionally large flowers. This is not a quality we particularly look for, but there is certainly a place for such roses and they are never in any way clumsy. They are of perfect deeply cupped formation, crisp and fresh in appearance, and of soft pink colouring. The growth is strong, about 3-3½ft. in height and bushy, so that the flowers do not appear out of proportion to the shrub. It repeats well for so large a flower and has a wonderful fragrance. Such blooms make an excellent statement in a bowl of mixed roses or other flowers. Breeding, 'Charles Austin' x seedling. Austin (U.K.), 1990. See page 139.

CANTERBURY. An almost single rose, bearing large wide open blooms of a lovely warm pink with a silky glowing quality and a fine boss of yellow stamens. Although this is one of the most beautiful single roses I know, it is rather weak, and the bush not quite large enough for the flowers. In spite of this, I feel it is well worth its place in the garden. It has a nice, spreading habit of growth, about 2½ft. in height. Fragrant. Breeding Hybrid Tea 'Monique' x ('Constance Spry' x seedling). Austin (U.K.), 1969.

CARDINAL HUME. I include this among the English Roses at the suggestion of the breeders, Harkness of Hitchin, because it has many of the characteristics of an English Rose. The flowers are small and held in sprays, and are of rich crimson-purple colouring, with a strong fruity fragrance. If they lack a little in form, the excellent habit of growth more than compensates for this. The only weakness of this rose is a tendency to blackspot. It blooms with exceptional continuity. Light fragrance. Harkness (U.K.), 1984.

CHARLES AUSTIN. A strong upright shrub with large shiny modern foliage and bearing exceptionally large, cupped, full-petalled flowers of an apricot-yellow colouring paling with age and becoming tinged with pink. Strong fruity fragrance. Although it does not repeat continuously, it can be relied on to provide a second crop in the autumn. It is perhaps a little coarse when put alongside our more recent productions, but can be very imposing towards the back of a border, where it will grow much taller if lightly pruned. For other positions it is better cut down to half its height if it is not to become ungainly. Height 4 to 6ft. Breeding 'Aloha' x 'Chaucer'. Austin (U.K.), 1973. See page 134.

CHARLES RENNIE MACKINTOSH.* Many people dislike the purple and lilac shades in modern roses, and certainly I do not find them attractive. They are often altogether too harsh and metallic. I do not feel the same about this rose. It is of a pleasing shade of lilac — a little to the lilac side of lilac-pink. The flower formation is cupped at first, opening wider. They have a somewhat frilly, feminine appearance that appeals to many people. The growth is tough and wiry, with plentiful thorns and dusky foliage. It mixes well with other colours, both in the house and in the garden. There is a strong fragrance. 3½ft. Breeding, 'Chaucer' x 'Conrad Ferdinand Meyer'. Austin (U.K.), 1988. See page 138.

CHARMIAN. Large, heavy rosette-shaped flowers of rich pink with a powerful Old Rose fragrance. These are carried on spreading rather floppy growth, similar to that of 'Lilian Austin', sometimes weighing down the branches to the ground. The height is usually about 4ft., but it will occasionally send up much taller growth. Breeding 'Lilian Austin' x unnamed seedling. Austin (U.K.), 1982. See page 149.

CHAUCER. A rose very much in the 'old' tradition. The leading flowers are quite large, deeply cupped and inclined to be of an enclosed chalice-like formation, while the side blooms will probably be more shallow, showing their stamens. Their colour is a light pink, paling towards the edges, and they have a strong myrrh fragrance. The growth is rather upright with small Gallica-like thorns and quite large, medium green foliage. Height 3½ft. The breeding of 'Chaucer' is interesting and a little surprising: 'Duchesse de Montebello' x 'Constance Spry', neither of which are repeat flowering. 'Constance Spry' has one repeat flowering parent, and it appears 'Duchesse de Montebello' must also have had one, otherwise it is unlikely these two parents would produce a recurrent-flowering seedling like 'Chaucer'. Austin (U.K.), 1970. See page 138.

CLAIRE ROSE. Large flowers of superb quality and perfect formation. They are of a delicate blush-pink at first and neatly cupped, opening by stages to a flat, many-petalled rosette which eventually recurves slightly and pales almost to white. The growth is strong and upright, with big, pale green leaves. A beautiful English Rose, the only fault being that the petals tend to spottle with age if there has been rain. It is then necessary to remove the offending blooms. Fragrant. 4 by 3ft. Named after my daughter, Claire. Austin (U.K.), 1986. See page 147.

* COTTAGE ROSE. For anyone who is looking for a good garden rose of truly Old Rose character that will flower throughout the summer, it would be hard to do better than use this variety. It produces charming,

COUNTRY LIVING, *one of the most charming of English Roses, with flowers of true Old Rose formation.*

CYMBELINE, *an English Rose which is almost grey in colour. Attractive arching growth.*

DOVE, *an English Rose with Tea Rose buds opening to rosette blooms; elegant spreading growth.*

DAPPLE DAWN, *English Rose. This rose and its parent 'Red Coat' are two of the most continuous flowering of all shrub roses.*

CHIANTI, *English Rose. The crimson counterpart of 'Constance Spry' with smaller flowers but better growth.*

medium-sized, rather cupped rosette flowers of a lovely warm pink. No sooner has one crop appeared, than numerous little branches are to be found all over the plant in readiness for the next crop. The flowers are pretty, but not very fragrant. Breeding, 'Wife of Bath' x 'Mary Rose'. Height 3½ ft. Austin (U.K.) 1991. See page 11.

* COUNTRY LIVING. An exquisite variety of typical Old Rose formation — in fact it might be said to be the epitome of a true Old Rose. The flowers are of the most delicate perfection and of a soft pink colouring which fades almost to white, with numerous short petals arranged into a perfect rosette. It will form a small shrub of twiggy, bushy character with small foliage and thorns. Some people have noticed a tendency for the growth to die back, rather in the manner of 'Wife of Bath'. We have not had this problem, but this should not matter as it will always shoot from the base. Fragrant. Height 3ft. The breeding was 'Wife of Bath' x 'Graham Thomas'. Austin (U.K.) 1991. See page 142.

CRESSIDA. Very large flowers of soft pink with apricot on the reverse of the petals, the two colours mingling to give a pleasing effect. The flowers are not easy to describe; they are of cupped formation with their petals arranged in an informal manner, giving them an almost artificial appearance, rather like the roses worn by Edwardian ladies, or like early Hybrid Teas that open full of petals. A vague description, but the best I can do! It does, however, illustrate the great variety of form that is possible in roses. 'Cressida' is the result of a cross between 'Conrad Ferdinand Meyer' and 'Chaucer', which may give some hint as to its appearance. It has the growth of its Rugosa parent, at least 6ft. in height, upright and perhaps a little clumsy, with many large thorns and large, rough-textured leaves. Strong myrrh scent. Austin (U.K.), 1983.

* CYMBELINE. Large flowers of 4ins. or more across, opening flat and loosely filled with petals. The colouring is most unusual, a greyish almost ashen pink with tinges of brown. Although this may not please everyone, I find it beautiful and think it could be useful in garden colour schemes, the growth arching to the ground in the most elegant manner and showing its flowers to maximum effect. It is truly recurrent flowering and has a strong myrrh fragrance. Height 4ft. Austin (U.K.), 1982. See page 142.

DAPPLE DAWN. I always find it difficult to know where to place the single English Roses. The justification for putting English Roses into a group is that they have flowers of the Old Rose formation, but the

DARK LADY, *an English Rose with spreading growth and large, attractively informal deep crimson flowers.*

singles could just as well go in with the class known, rather vaguely, as Modern Shrubs. Here we have a good example of this. 'Dapple Dawn' is a sport from 'Red Coat', see below. The flowers are large, 4 or 5ins. across, and held well apart in open sprays. They are delicate pink, veined all over with a stronger pink and have long yellow stamens. The petals are quite thin, giving them at times a gossamer-like quality, but it is the overall effect that is so pleasing. To see this variety planted in

ENGLISH ELEGANCE, *an English Rose with intriguing colours, elegant growth and large flowers.*

a group, with its flowers held so daintily above the foliage, can be an enchanting sight. Like 'Red Coat' it is an excellent shrub and hardly ever without flowers. Light fragrance. Austin (U.K.), 1983. See page 143.

* DARK LADY. This is the result of a cross between the English Roses 'Mary Rose' and 'Prospero', but, with the exception of its dark colouring, it seems to have followed the former parent. Its flowers are larger than 'Mary Rose', but have something of the same informal character which, in this case, gives it a particular attraction. The growth tends to be low and spreading, holding the blooms in the most graceful manner. There is a strong Old Rose fragrance. Height 3ft. The name was taken from Shakespeare's Dark Lady of the Sonnets. Austin (U.K.) 1991. See page 145.

DOVE. A small spreading shrub of about 2½ ft. in height and 3ft. across. The flowers lean towards those of a Tea Rose, but only at the bud stage. They are of pointed formation, opening out into a nice rosette shape. Their colour is white tinged with dusky blush. It is the graceful nature of its growth together with the elegant poise of the flowers that provide its particular beauty. The foliage is dark green and of the pointed Musk Rose type. There is a fresh, apple fragrance. All in all a pretty little shrub fitting nicely into the front of the border. Breeding 'Wife of Bath' x (unnamed seedling x 'Iceberg'). Austin (U.K.), 1984. See page 143.

EMANUEL. Large, heavy, voluptuous flowers of a soft blush-pink shaded with gold at the base. They open to a rather flat bloom made up of numerous petals which are twisted and scrolled at the centre in an unusual manner, the colours mingling to create a most attractive effect. Rich fragrance. The growth is vigorous, some 4ft. in height, and it is

CLAIRE ROSE, *English Rose. Large blooms of pleasing shallow cupped formation.*

A GARDEN OF *English Roses at David Austin Rose Nurseries. 'Perdita' is at the front; the yellow rose is 'Graham Thomas'.*

exceptionally free flowering. The only weakness is a tendency to blackspot and it may require spraying in areas subject to this disease. This rose was named for David and Elizabeth Emanuel, the well-known dress designers. Austin (U.K.), 1985.

EMILY. There are some roses that one is rather doubtful about introducing to the general public, and 'Emily' is such a rose. The growth and vigour leaves a little to be desired. However, the flowers are

EMILY, *English Rose. Not a large rose, but of unique and beautiful formation.*

CHARMIAN, *a medium-sized English Rose with large flowers and a strong fragrance.*

FAIR BIANCA, *an English Rose producing most perfect medium-sized flowers on a short bush.*

of such delicacy and charm that we felt it would be a shame not to make it available. The blooms commence as attractive buds and the outer petals open wide, leaving the inner petals in a cupped formation at the centre — almost like a cup and saucer. Gradually these too fall back to form a cupped rosette, still leaving the outer petals hanging down. The outer petals are almost white, while the inner petals are a glowing blush-pink. A perfectly satisfactory rose as long as it is well fed and looked after. There is a strong fragrance. Height 2½ ft. The breeding is 'The Prioress' x 'Mary Rose'. Austin (U.K.) 1992.

ENGLISH ELEGANCE. Quite large flowers, opening wide, the outer ring of petals retaining their form, while the numerous inner petals twist and turn in all directions to give a most attractive effect. The colour is difficult to describe: the outer petals are blush, gradually becoming pink, then a rich clear salmon-pink towards the centre; at the same time the backs of the petals are shaded with gold which becomes mixed with the other colours, resulting in an ever-changing effect as they unfold. The growth is strong but graceful, 4 to 5ft. in height, with long stems bending slightly outwards and bearing well-spaced sprays of bloom. Austin (U.K.), 1986. See page 146.

EVELYN, *one of the most beautiful and fragrant of all English Roses*

* ENGLISH GARDEN. Rosette shaped flowers of about 3½ins. across, with numerous small petals forming an almost perfect example of an Old Rose. The colour is buff-yellow, paling towards the edges. The growth is not very shrubby, but short and upright, about 3ft. in height, with light green leaves. When well grown there are few English Roses that can match its flowers for symmetry of form. Pleasant Tea Rose fragrance. Breeding ('Lilian Austin' x unnamed seedling) x ('Iceberg' x 'Wife of Bath'). Austin (U.K.), 1986.

* EVELYN. One of the most magnificent English Roses we have bred. The flowers are unusually large and open to form a perfect cup filled with numerous perfectly placed petals, which gradually recurve to form a rosette-shaped bloom. Their colouring is a lovely mixture of apricot and yellow. 'Evelyn' belongs to the same successful line as 'Jayne Austin' and 'Sweet Juliet', which are closely related to the Noisette Rose 'Gloire de Dijon', and we can see the influence of this famous old rose in its flowers. It was introduced in association with Crabtree & Evelyn, the well known perfumers and, as befits its name, it has a particularly strong and delicious fragrance. In fact, we regard 'Evelyn' and 'Gertrude Jekyll' as being two of the most fragrant of all roses. The growth is perhaps a little rigid — about 3½ft. or so in height — but this is a small price to pay for so beautiful a flower. Breeding, 'Graham Thomas' x 'Tamora'. Austin (U.K.) 1991. See page 151.

GRAHAM THOMAS, *an individual bloom of this fine English Rose.*

ENGLISH GARDEN, *English Rose. Neatly formed medium to large flowers on a short bush.*

153

⇒ See page 150.

FAIR BIANCA. A small upright shrub of 3ft. in height, with something of the appearance of a Gallica Rose. The flowers are of the most exquisite Old Rose formation, and of purest white. They are in the form of a neatly sculptured, shallow cup packed with small petals. There is a button eye at the centre and, in the middle of this, the greenish dot of its stigma can be seen. It has small light green leaves and thin spiny thorns. There is a strong fragrance of myrrh. It would be no exaggeration to say that the flowers come close to 'Madame Hardy' for sheer perfection of form. The general character of both flower and bush goes right back to 'Belle Isis', which was one of the original crosses. A useful rose for the small garden. Austin (U.K.), 1982. See page 150.

FINANCIAL TIMES CENTENARY. Large, fragrant, globular blooms of the clearest, purest pink imaginable. The growth tends to be distinctly upright, which some people might regard as a disadvantage, although it can be very useful when grown behind other roses or plants. It has a pleasant fragrance. Height 3½ ft. Named for the one hundredth anniversary of *The Financial Times.* Breeding, 'Seedling' x 'Seedling'. Austin (U.K.), 1988.

FISHERMAN'S FRIEND. Quite large, full-petalled flowers, cupped at first, later forming an attractive rosette — the colour varying from deep garnet-red to deep cerise-crimson as the flower ages. The growth is

Right: FRANCINE AUSTIN, *English Rose. A dainty Noisette hybrid, with the long, wiry stems, nicely spaced flowers and sheeny petals of its parent. A small shrub with elegant, arching growth.*

Left: HERO, *English Rose. Cupped flowers of exceptional purity of colour.*

strong and thorny with deep green, rough textured foliage, which relates back to *Rosa rugosa*. This is an excellent tough rose which has been found to be exceptionally hardly in the Canadian climate, but has an unfortunate tendency to blackspot in England. Strong fragrance. 3½ ft. 'Lilian Austin' x 'The Squire'. Austin (U.K.), 1987.

* FRANCINE AUSTIN. We bred this rose by crossing the beautiful Noisette Rose 'Alister Stella Gray' with 'Ballerina', one of the most reliable of all Modern Shrub Roses. The result is a medium-sized shrub of pleasing, arching growth, bearing sprays of small, pure white flowers. It could therefore reasonably be considered a ground-cover rose. I mention it here, as it has retained much of the refinement of the old Noisette Roses. As with the Noisettes, the flowers are held on thin, wiry stems, well apart from each other in dainty sprays. It flowers freely and continuously — its long branches often wreathed with white, providing a lovely picture. The foliage is pale green — the leaves being made up of long leaflets. Height 3 to 4ft. and as much across. It is named after my daughter-in-law. Austin (U.K.), 1988. See page 155.

PRETTY JESSICA, *English Rose. A short grower for the smaller garden.*

GERTRUDE JEKYLL, *English Rose. Exceptionally fragrant flowers of true Old Rose character. Strong and reliable.*

* GERTRUDE JEKYLL. In the breeding of the English Roses there has always been a danger that, as the generations pass, we should imperceptibly slip back towards the Hybrid Tea and Floribunda. The genes that control repeat flowering are closely linked with these roses, and when we select for the repeat-flowering characteristic in English Roses there is a tendency to bring along much of the character of the modern rose as well. If we let this happen we lose the 'old' characteristics that are the essential purpose of English Roses. It is with this in mind that I have, from time to time, back-crossed to Old Roses. This rose is a cross between the English Rose 'Wife of Bath' and the old Portland Rose 'Comte de Chambord'.

'Gertrude Jekyll' is a rich, deep, warm-pink colour, sometimes almost red in cool weather, with pretty buds not unlike those of the charming Alba 'Celestial'. These develop, almost surprisingly, into substantial

GLAMIS CASTLE, *a white English Rose that flowers with exceptional continuity.*

GOLDEN CELEBRATION, *a superb golden-yellow English Rose with giant flowers and graceful growth.*

well-filled rosettes with the petals spiralling from the centre, often with the most perfect precision. The flowers are quite large, although occasionally we get a giant bloom on the end of a very strong main shoot. Above all, the fragrance is particularly powerful — the true Damask fragrance of its Portland Rose parent. It is very much the Old Rose, with strong affinities to its Portland Rose parent. It has, in fact, been chosen to be grown commercially to produce the first rose perfume to be manufactured in this country for 250 years. I can think of no other rose with quite so strong a fragrance. Height 5ft. Gertrude Jekyll, as most of my readers will know, was one of the great influences in English gardening, and was the author of a beautiful book on roses, *Roses for English Gardens.* Austin (U.K.), 1986. See page 157.

* GLAMIS CASTLE. We regard this as the best white rose we have bred to date. It bears flowers of cupped formation and typical Old Rose character and charm. Sometimes there is just a tinge of buff at the centre of the flower as it opens. There is a strong myrrh fragrance. The growth is short and bushy with numerous twiggy shoots, and the

7? JAYNE AUSTIN, *English Rose. A beautiful rose, showing a Noisette influence in its delicate, sheeny-petalled flowers.*

GRAHAM THOMAS, *English Rose. Cupped flowers in a good shade of yellow. Strong tea fragrance.*

flowers are produced with exceptional freedom and continuity, making it ideal both as a border rose and for bedding. Many people say that it blooms with more freedom and continuity than the average Floribunda. It is the result of a cross between 'Graham Thomas' and 'Mary Rose'. No doubt it gains its excellent habit of growth and freedom of flowering from 'Mary Rose'. Height 3ft.

Glamis Castle is the family home of the Earls of Strathmore and Kinghorne and has been a royal residence since 1372. It is the childhood home of the Queen Mother, the birthplace of Princess Margaret and the legendary setting of Shakespeare's play *Macbeth*. The castle is one of the most historic in Britain. Austin (U.K.), 1992.

* GOLDEN CELEBRATION. This variety is turning out to be one of the very best of the English Roses, partly because of its superb large golden-yellow cup-shaped flowers which can achieve as much as 5ins. across, but no less for its excellent habit of growth. The blooms are held on elegant, slightly arching stems and the shrub itself is neatly rounded. The foliage is a light glossy green, which goes perfectly with the colour of the flowers. It is very strong and healthy and reliable in every way. Richly fragrant. Breeding 'Charles Austin' x 'Abraham Darby'. Height 4ft. Austin (U.K.), 1992. See paged 159.

* GRAHAM THOMAS. This is one of the best English Roses up to the present time. It has flowers of the richest and purest deep yellow colouring, a shade which would be difficult to match in any other rose, certainly in any other Shrub Rose. In the early stages there is just a hint of apricot. This variety, a little to my surprise, came from a cross between 'Charles Austin' and a hybrid between 'Iceberg' and an English Rose. I had hoped for yellow seedlings, but did not expect a colour of such richness and purity — a colour unequalled even among Modern Roses. The flowers are of deeply-cupped formation, chaliced at first and opening wider, the petals mingling loosely within. They are of medium size, although they sometimes produce an exceptionally large bloom at the centre of a spray. They have a strong Tea Rose fragrance which I am particularly pleased to have among the English Roses. The growth is very strong, breaking freely at almost every joint as well as at the base to produce further flowers. The leaves are smooth and reminiscent of those of 'Iceberg'. If we look for faults we might say that the growth is a little too upright and narrow at the base, although it is quite bushy and, as Graham Thomas himself asks: 'Too upright for what?' It grows to 4ft. in height. Rather oddly, I have received a report from South Africa that it grows to some 10ft. in height there in the manner of a Climber, although I have no similar reports from other countries. Such variations are not uncommon when roses are grown in different parts of the world, although this example is rather extreme. Austin (U.K.), 1983. See pages 152 and 161.

GRUSS AN AACHEN. I have taken the liberty of placing this beautiful Old Rose in this section. Bred by F. Geduldig of Germany in 1909, long before the English Roses were thought of, it is so close to the English Rose ideal that I can think of no better section in which to place it. It arose from a cross between 'Frau Karl Druschki' and the Polyantha Rose 'Franz Deegen', and bears little relationship to any previous class of roses, forming a bushy plant of 3ft. in height with large, cupped

HERITAGE *bears some of the most perfect blooms of any English Rose and is also a very good shrub.*

GRUSS AN AACHEN, *a rose of English type with charming cupped flowers.*

flowers of a pearly-pink colour fading with age to creamy-white. They are full petalled and of typical Old Rose character, with a lovely silky sheen and delicious fragrance. In addition to this it is truly repeat flowering and, as one would expect from its parentage, very tough and hardy. See page 164.

 * HERITAGE. This is one of the most beautiful English Roses. The flowers are of medium size and of a most perfect cupped formation. Their colour is a soft blush-pink, and the petals within the cup are each placed with exquisite perfection, giving it a shell-like beauty. The flowers are produced in small — though sometimes large — sprays and have a strong fragrance with just a hint of lemon. It has smooth stems, few thorns and pointed Hybrid Musk Rose foliage. In growth and leaf 'Heritage' has much in common with the rose 'Graham Thomas', but owes more to its 'Iceberg' ancestor. It is branching and bushy, breaking freely along the stem to produce further flowers. It forms a nice, shapely rounded shrub of 4 or 5ft. in height. The breeding was an unnamed English seedling x ('Wife of Bath' x 'Iceberg'). Austin (U.K.), 1984. See page 163.

HERO. A rather straggly shrub, its long branches shooting out in a loose and open manner. The problem is that the growth is not sufficiently full to form a shapely shrub on its own, so it is necessary to plant two or three close together to achieve a good overall effect; on the other hand, the flowers are of a pink of quite unusual warmth and purity, a colour rare among repeat-flowering Shrub Roses. The earlier blooms are in the form of large, open cups and are often very fine, but later in the season they may be of more shallow formation. The flowers are held widely spaced in small sprays and have a strong myrrh fragrance. The height is about 5ft. spreading to almost as much across. The foliage is smooth, and there are a few large thorns. Austin (U.K.), 1982. See page 154.

* JAYNE AUSTIN. If the reader will refer to the description of Tamora in this chapter, he will be able to understand the derivation of this rose. 'Jayne Austin' results from a cross between 'Graham Thomas' and 'Tamora', and may be said to represent the Noisette branch of the English Roses, as opposed to the majority which are related to the old

LUCETTA, *English Rose. A medium-sized shrub of excellent habit of growth and repeating well.*

L.D. BRAITHWAITE, *English Rose. An excellent small shrub with bright, unfading crimson flowers. It blooms continuously.*

Shrub Roses.

It is truly a beautiful rose, as our picture shows. The flowers are shallowly cupped at first, later becoming rosette shaped. In colour they are yellow, tending a little towards apricot — the outer petals being paler, and their petals have the lovely silky sheen that we find in the Noisette Roses and their descendants. The excellent growth of this rose owes much to 'Graham Thomas'; the growth being slender and upright, with the same ability to branch and repeat flower continuously. The leaves are plentiful and pale green. It has a wonderful Tea Rose fragrance. A very charming rose. Height 3½ft. Austin (U.K.), 1990. See page 160.

* KATHRYN MORLEY. A dainty rose with medium-sized, prettily-cupped flowers of clear pink colouring. These are numerous and repeat with admirable regularity throughout the summer. The growth is bushy and there is a good fragrance. All these virtues make it a very satisfactory garden rose. The name was auctioned at The Variety Club of Great Britain in aid of The Shaftesbury Homes, raising £13,000. It

LILIAN AUSTIN *is less of an Old Rose than most English Roses, but it is an ideal shrub for the border.*

was named after Mr. and Mrs. Eric Morley's daughter, who died after a long illness at the age of seventeen. Breeding, 'Mary Rose' x 'Chaucer'. Austin (U.K.), 1990.

* L.D. BRAITHWAITE. 'Mary Rose' (see below) is a most satisfactory shrub. It has pleasing bushy growth and repeats particularly well. 'The Squire' has the most superb deep crimson flowers, but rather unsatisfactory growth. 'L.D. Braithwaite' combines these virtues while avoiding the weaknesses, thus providing us with perhaps the most satisfactory red rose in this group. This is most pleasing, as good red roses are notoriously difficult to obtain. It forms a low, rather spreading shrub of about 3ft. in height, is seldom without flowers, and its colour is a bright crimson which is slow to fade. The flowers are nicely, if a little loosely, formed, and fragrant. Austin (U.K.), 1988. See page 166.

LILAC ROSE. Quite a different rose to 'Charles Rennie Mackintosh', though of similar lilac colouring. The flowers are large, flat and rosette shaped, and have an exceptionally strong fragrance. The growth is bushy and upright, about 2½ft. in height. Breeding, seedling x 'Hero'. Austin (U.K.), 1990.

* LILIAN AUSTIN. This rose lacks something of the Old Rose character which we look for in English Roses. It is, however, a first class small garden shrub of an excellent, spreading, bushy habit and one which looks very much in place with other plants in the border. The flowers are semi-double, at times almost double, but showing their stamens, while their petals are slightly waved. The colour is a strong salmon-pink, shading to yellow at the centre. 'Lilian Austin' is hardy, disease resistant, and reliably repeat flowering and it has a good fragrance. Breeding, 'Aloha' and 'The Yeoman'. Austin (U.K.), 1973. See page 167.

* LUCETTA. Very large, flat, semi-double, saucer-like flowers of a soft blush-pink, becoming paler with age, with a large boss of stamens. This is a particularly good shrub; healthy and strong growing, to about 5ft. in height and as much across, with long arching branches. The great blooms are nicely poised and contrast well with its ample, dark green foliage. It is seldom without flowers and is in every way tough and reliable. Fragrant. Parentage not known. Austin (U.K.), 1983. See page 165.

* MARY ROSE. This rose was introduced at the Chelsea Flower Show in 1983 and, together with 'Graham Thomas', received a lot of attention

MARY ROSE *is an excellent, reliable English Rose that flowers continuously.*

PERDITA, *English Rose. One of the best all round varieties.*

from the media, which did much to make the English Roses known to a wider public. It is not at first sight startling, but has a modest charm. The flowers are quite large, informally cupped, and loosely filled with petals, their colour a strong rose-pink that may be paler in the autumn. They are only slightly fragrant. 'Mary Rose' forms a very good shrub of about 4ft. in height with foliage close to that of an Old Rose. It is quite thorny. The great virtue of this rose lies in its bushy, branching habit of growth. It combines this with a truly Old Rose character. This is a difficult combination to achieve and this rose is, I am pleased to say, passing all these qualities on to its progeny. When mass planted the pink of the flowers blends most effectively with the green of its leaves. It is very tough and can be pruned hard or allowed to grow into a larger shrub. The result of a cross between 'Wife of Bath' and 'The Miller'. Named on behalf of The Mary Rose Trust, to mark the recovery of Henry VIII's famous flagship from the Solent after more than four hundred years. Austin (U.K.), 1983.

MARY WEBB. Of all shades of yellow to be found among roses a soft lemon is perhaps the most pleasing and suitable. This rose has flowers of just such a colour; they are large and cupped with loosely arranged petals. The growth is strong and bushy, with ample large, pale green

PEACH BLOSSOM, *English Rose. Masses of flowers, giving a delicate blossom-like effect.*

foliage. Perhaps it might be said that the flowers are a little indefinite in form and character. There is a very strong fragrance. It is named after the novelist and poet who lived not far from our nurseries. Austin (U.K.), 1984.

OTHELLO. An unusual variety. The blooms are very large — larger than most others in this group, deeply cupped in shape and very full with numerous petals. As it varies so much the exact colour is difficult to describe: most often it is a deep crimson that quickly turns to crimson-purple, at other times it will take on lighter shades in all but the outer petals. Often there is a most attractive combination of tints. These flowers are of a rough-hewn appearance, sometimes appearing a little coarse. They have the deep, powerful fragrance that seems so right for this type of flower. The growth is very strong, upright but bushy, 4ft. or more in height, with numerous strong thorns and dark green foliage. It repeats very well for such a large flower. There is some tendency to mildew, although not so much as to cause great concern. The parents were 'Lilian Austin' and 'The Squire'. Austin (U.K.), 1986.

SAINT CECILIA, *an English Rose with short but elegant growth and dainty cupped flowers.*

* PEACH BLOSSOM. Here we have a rose of supreme delicacy and refinement. Although the blooms are quite large, they are produced very freely and nicely poised on airy growth. They are of sheeny pink colouring, and their massed effect does, to me at least, have a blossom-like quality. A good shrubby rose of 4ft. in height. It is the result of a cross between 'The Prioress' and 'Mary Rose'. Austin (U.K.), 1990. See page 171.

* PERDITA. A good small shrub, with bushy, slightly arching growth to about 3½ft. constantly shooting from the base and providing continuity of bloom. The flowers are fully double, of medium size, delicate apricot-blush in colour and of shallowly-dished, rather cupped formation. It has ample, dark green disease-free foliage and red-brown stems, the growth generally leaning towards that of the Modern Rose. The fragrance is strong, not unlike that of a Tea Rose, and it was awarded the Royal National Rose Society's Henry Edland Medal for fragrance in 1984. Its parents were 'The Friar' x (unnamed seedling x 'Iceberg'). Austin (U.K.), 1983. See page 170.

POTTER AND MOORE. This is a descendant of 'Wife of Bath', one of the most successful of our earlier varieties, and it may be regarded as an improvement on that rose. It has the same toughness and freedom of flowering, but the individual blooms are finer and more full. The colour is a similar shade of soft pink. Its disadvantage is a tendency for the flowers to be spoiled by damp weather. A typical Old Rose flower with a pleasant fragrance. Height 3ft. Breeding, 'Wife of Bath' x seedling. Austin (U.K.), 1988.

PRETTY JESSICA. A very small bush, no more than 2½ft. in height, of upright growth, and ideal for anyone who has only a small garden yet would like to have a rose of truly Old Rose character. The flowers are shallow, cup shaped and very full, and have a delicious Old Rose fragrance, while their colour is that rich, warm, glowing pink which we associate with the Centifolias. The foliage is somewhat sparse and not very resistant to disease. A charming little rose that flowers repeatedly, it was a hybrid between 'Wife of Bath' and an unnamed seedling. Austin (U.K.), 1983. See page 156.

PROSPERO. This variety is capable of bearing blooms of the very highest Old Rose perfection. They are medium size and their colour is deepest rich crimson eventually turning to pleasing shades of purple and mauve. Their form is faultless, opening flat or slightly domed with numerous small petals. There is also a strong Old Rose fragrance. Here, unfortunately, the virtues end, for 'Prospero' is of a rather weak constitution and only when grown on good land with generous

PROSPERO, *an English Rose with perfectly formed crimson rosettes. Short growth.*

treatment will it achieve the standard described above. A rose for the enthusiast. Height 2ft. Breeding, 'The Knight' x 'Château de Clos Vougeot'. Austin (U.K.), 1982.

QUEEN NEFERTITI. Medium-sized blooms of rosette formation and soft yellow colouring, with just a hint of apricot. The growth is short, bushy and tough, branching very freely to produce exceptionally continuous flowering. Fragrant. Height 3ft. Breeding, 'Lilian Austin' x 'Tamora'. Austin (U.K.), 1988.

RED COAT. The parent of 'Dapple Dawn' described above: its red flowers seem to be of slightly greater substance, otherwise it is similar. The colour appears rather harsh when the flowers are viewed individually; this is a nice fresh scarlet-crimson at first, but later it hardens to a duller shade. It is, however, when seen in the mass, however, that 'Red Coat' is most impressive — the whole effect is as though a multitude of butterflies had descended upon the bushes, and this is particularly noticeable in the nursery fields. I have often wished I could persuade municipal planters to use this rose, for I can think of few varieties more suitable for massed effect. In studying 'Red Coat' and 'Dapple Dawn' at regular intervals throughout the summer, we have found them to be hardly ever without bloom, and with the exception of 'Ballerina' I know of no other roses so consistent in this respect. 'Red Coat' may be pruned as a bush when it will grow to about 4ft. in height, or as a shrub, which will achieve 5 or 6ft. There is little scent. 'Parade' x an English Rose. Austin (U.K.), 1973.

* REDOUTÉ. This is a sport from the ever-popular 'Mary Rose', to which it is identical except for the fact that its flowers are of a soft shade of pink — the kind of pink one finds in the Alba Roses. In my opinion, the individual flowers are more beautiful in this shade. Otherwise, it has all the good qualities of its parent. It is free-flowering, repeats well and forms a good shapely, bushy, twiggy shrub. Light fragrance. Height 4ft. Pierre Joseph Redouté was the most famous of all rose painters. His work included some 170 varieties from the Empress Josephine's garden at Malmaison. Austin (U.K.) 1992.

* SAINT CECILIA. A small, low-growing shrub of excellent bushy habit. The flowers are medium size, of a nice deep cupped shape and pale buff-apricot colouring. It is the manner in which these are held on the bush which gives St. Cecilia its particular attraction. They are nicely poised on long, slightly arching stems, with each flower placed sufficiently apart from its neighbour. All these qualities go together to provide us with a small but elegant shrub.

REDOUTÉ, *English Rose. A sport from 'Mary Rose', in a softer and perhaps more pleasing pink.*

The flowers appear in extended succession, and it is not long before new shoots appear to enable them to continue well in the autumn. The leaves and thorns are small, tending towards an Old Rose in appearance. There is a strong demand for small shrubs of this type, and this charming little rose has proved popular, particularly with those who have small gardens. Myrrh fragrance. A seedling from 'Wife of Bath', it has inherited much of the reliability of that rose. Austin ((U.K.), 1987. See page 172.

SHARIFA ASMA. I know of few roses that can compare with this for the sheer delicacy and charm of the individual bloom. They are of full rosette shape, with delicate but weather-resistant petals of soft blush-pink colouring. The growth is not over strong but quite adequate,

SIR WALTER RALEIGH, *English Rose. Giant flowers, like those of a tree peony.*

SWAN, *English Rose. Large perfectly formed rosette flowers, tall upright growth.*

forming a small bush of fairly upright growth. It has a strong fragrance. Height 3½ft. Breeding 'Mary Rose' x 'Admired Miranda'. Austin (U.K.), 1989. See Frontispiece.

SIR CLOUGH. This variety was the result of a cross between 'Chaucer' and the Rugosa 'Conrad Ferdinand Meyer', but leans much more towards the Rugosa parent; indeed it could easily be included in that class. 'Sir Clough' forms a large shrub of perhaps 6ft. in height, with many thorns and dark, rough-textured leaves. The flowers are semi-double, of an unusual and beautiful shade of cerise-pink, rather informal in shape with contrasting stamens and a delicious fragrance. The growth is tough and hardy. Named after Sir Clough Williams-Ellis, the architect, best known as the designer of Portmeirion in North Wales. Austin (U.K.), 1983.

SIR EDWARD ELGAR. The chief attraction of this rose is its beautiful cerise-crimson colour. This is of a shade that is difficult to reproduce in a photograph, and equally difficult to put into words. It also varies very considerably, being most beautiful on a hot day. The flowers are large and cup-shaped at first, later recurving to form a nice shapely bloom. The growth is perhaps a little more upright than one would like. Light fragrance. Height 3½ft. Breeding 'Mary Rose' x 'The Squire'. Named

176

on behalf of The Elgar Society, in honour of the famous composer. Austin (U.K.), 1992.

SIR WALTER RALEIGH. A large and generous rose, the result of a cross between 'Lilian Austin' and 'Chaucer'. The flowers are rather like those of a tree peony, at least 5ins. across, not quite fully double, opening wide and slightly cupped, usually showing their stamens. They are a lovely warm pink and have a strong Old Rose fragrance. The growth is tall and strong, about 5ft. high by 4ft. across, the foliage large, with everything in proportion to the flowers. This is perhaps the nearest we have to a repeat-flowering 'Constance Spry', although the flowers are less full. Named to mark the four hundredth anniversary of the founding of the first English speaking colony in America. Austin (U.K.), 1985.

SIR EDWARD ELGAR, *an English rose notable for its colour — an unusual and pleasing light red that it is hard to capture in a picture.*

SWAN. A strong shrub of similar growth to 'Charles Austin', having the same large, rather modern foliage and tall, upright growth. The flowers at their best are magnificent, being large, white with a slight tinge of buff, rosette shaped and perfectly formed. Their only weakness is a tendency to become spotted in wet weather — a frequent problem with white roses. 'Swan' repeats satisfactorily but, like 'Charles Austin', it may require cutting back to half way in order to prevent it becoming too lanky. Fragrant. Breeding 'Charles Austin' x (unnamed seedling x 'Iceberg'). Austin (U.K.), 1987. See page 176.

* SWEET JULIET. Very similar to 'Jayne Austin', which I have already described, having the same medium-sized, shallow, saucer-shaped flowers, but of apricot-yellow colouring. These, though beautiful, are a little less perfect, with an occasional tendency to split. It is of similar breeding, with a strong Noisette influence resulting in prolific growth. Strong Tea scent. Height 3½ft. Breeding, 'Graham Thomas' x 'Admired Miranda'. Austin (U.K.), 1989. See page 180.

SYMPHONY. At its best, this rose bears attractive rosette shaped blooms of soft yellow colouring. These have a tendency to turn pink at the edges as they age, and this robs them of some of their beauty. It is, however, a reliable little shrub — very free and continuous flowering — which may also be used as a bedding rose. Fragrant. 3½ft. 'The Knight' x Floribunda 'Yellow Cushion' Austin (U.K.), 1986.

TAMORA. A cross beteween 'Chaucer' and 'Conrad Ferdinand Meyer' which has resulted in a short bush, bearing cupped flowers of apricot colouring, with silky textured petals and myrrh fragrance. It appears to have drawn all its character from 'Chaucer' and 'Souvenir de la Malmaison', which was one parent of 'Conrad Ferdinand Meyer', leaving no trace of the Rugosa side of the latter rose. It is a nice little rose but has now been largely superseded by 'Jayne Austin' and 'Sweet Juliet'. 3ft. Austin (U.K.), 1983.

* THE COUNTRYMAN. Like Gertrude Jekyll this is a cross between an English Rose and a Portland Rose,and it may be helpful to refer back to my remarks on 'Gertrude Jekyll'. Here we have a cross between 'Lilian Austin' and 'Comte de Chambord'. It is shorter than 'Gertrude Jekyll', perhaps 3ft. in height, the growth bending over and taking on the excellent arching habit of 'Lilian Austin'. The flowers are quite large, loosely double rosettes, deep pink in colour, with an exceptional Old Rose fragrance. For me, they have something of the spirit of the peonies we see in Chinese and Japanese paintings, both in character and the way in which they grow on the plant, although they are, in

reality, much smaller. The leaves have something of the character of a Portland, quite large with well spaced leaflets. It is important to remove the dead flowers to encourage quick new growth, and we can then expect two good periods of flower, although there will only be occasional blooms in between. Austin (U.K.), 1987. See page 180.

THE HERBALIST. We chose this name because this rose, superficially at least, bears a likeness to the Gallica 'Officinalis' (the 'Apothecaries' Rose'). It has similar strong pink colouring and semi-double flowers, opening flat with golden stamens. The growth is nice and bushy, and the repeat-flowering good. This is not a showy rose, but it has a simple beauty and is ideal for growing in a mixed border. Breeding, 'Seedling' x 'Louise Odier'. Austin (U.K.), 1991. See page 181.

THE NUN. Not all roses should be introduced with a peal of bells or in the hope that they will one day rate among the most popular of roses. Some may be of more modest ambition. This is such a rose. It is a seedling from 'The Prioress', with flowers of similar open-cupped formation, and almost pure white. This form is pushed a little further with 'The Nun', the stamens being visible within, almost like a tulip, which I think is a very desirable shape of flower. The difficulty is that the petals do not always remain rigid — one or two of them may fall inwards to cover the stamens, and this can happen with 'The Nun'. At its best, this is a beautiful rose, its flowers held well apart in open sprays, giving an effect of dainty purity. Slight scent. Austin (U.K.), 1987.

* THE PILGRIM. This is perhaps the most strong, healthy and reliable of the English Roses, bearing flowers of the utmost delicacy and charm. These form quite large, evenly shaped rosettes which are filled with numerous small petals of soft yellow colouring. Indeed, the whole flower has a softness of texture which is most pleasing. They are particularly beautiful when arranged in a bowl. This variety has an interesting peculiarity which I think is unique (although I am sure there is someone who can tell me otherwise): the flower stems can occasionally be noticed not only breaking out from the leaf joints as is usual, but also coming from the bare stem. It is as though it was so impatient to produce flowers, that it sometimes does so in unlikely places! Indeed, it is an extremely free-flowering rose. Breeding 'Graham Thomas' x 'Yellow Button'. Height 3½ ft. Austin (U.K.) 1991. See page 7.

* THE PRINCE. The outstanding feature of this rose is its almost unqiue colouring — a deep rich crimson which quickly turns to a remarkable and equally rich royal purple, a shade of purple found in one or two

THE COUNTRYMAN, *English Rose. An interesting back-cross to a Portland Rose, with low arching growth and fragrant flowers of true Old Rose character.*

SWEET JULIET, *a beautiful, free flowering, reliable English Rose.*

THE PRINCE, *English Rose. Richest crimson turning to richest purple; unique amongst present day roses.*

THE HERBALIST, *English Rose. Not unlike the Gallica Rose 'Officinalis', but repeat-flowering.*

early Gallicas, but not to be found in any later rose, and almost impossible to catch in a photograph. 'The Prince' is the result of a cross between 'Lilian Austin' and 'The Squire' and no doubt gains its excellent neatly spreading habit of growth from the former and its colour from the latter. The foliage leans towards the Modern Rose, and it has an exceptionally Old Rose fragrance. Height 2-2½ft. Austin (U.K.), 1990. See page 181.

THE REEVE. This rose has flowers of deeply cupped formation, the petals tending to incurve, sometimes forming an almost completely enclosed globe. The colour is a very dark pink and there is a powerful Old Rose fragrance. The growth is wide, unusually lax and arching, about 2½ft. in height, the leaves dark green and the stems covered with thorns. The whole effect is one of dusky darkness. 'The Reeve' is perhaps best when planted in groups of two, three, or more, which will then form a sprawling mass. It would, no doubt, provide a pleasing picture if trained over a low retaining wall. Unlike any other rose I know. A cross between 'Lilian Austin' and 'Chaucer'. Austin (U.K.), 1979. See page 185.

THE SQUIRE. I know of no deep crimson rose that produces such superb blooms as 'The Squire'. Unfortunately it is a sparse grower and very subject to disease. Those who grow it should bear these facts in mind. The flowers are very large, deep, full cups, very fragrant and of the richest, darkest crimson imaginable. Rough textured, dark green foliage. Height 3ft. Breeding, 'The Knight' x 'Chateau de Clos Vougeot'. Austin (U.K.), 1977.

WARWICK CASTLE. 'Lilian Austin' is a particularly good garden shrub, but the flowers are of a modern type, though not necessarily any the worse for this. It is of bushy, spreading growth and repeat flowers well. 'Warwick Castle' is a cross between 'Lilian Austin' and 'The Reeve'. The result is a rose with many of the qualities of 'Lilian Austin', but with full-petalled Old Rose flowers. They are of flat formation, 3½ins. across, with many small petals, and have a strong rose-pink colouring. It will grow into a good small shrub of some 3ft. in height, with slender, arching stems spreading wide to form mound-like growth, while continually pushing up new shoots from the base to give continuity of flowering. Very fragrant, though with a tendency to blackspot in some seasons. This rose was named to commemorate the opening of the beautiful Victorian rose garden at Warwick Castle (a replica of the original designed by Robert Marnock in 1868) which is well worth a visit. Austin (U.K.), 1986.

WENLOCK. This has proved to be a good and reliable red rose of shrubby growth, about 4ft. in height. The colour might be described as a medium crimson, which turns to cerise with age. The flowers are large shallow cups loosely filled with petals. They are produced with the greatest freedom and have a strong fragrance. 'L.D. Braithwaite' is of better colour and more pleasing growth. 'Wenlock' was bred from a cross between 'The Knight' and 'Glastonbury'. Austin (U.K.), 1984.

* WIFE OF BATH. A charming little rose, forming a bushy, twiggy shrub 3ft. in height. The flowers are of medium size, starting as pretty little tightly-petalled cups of warm pink, and gradually opening into more loosely-petalled open cups which are clear pink at the centre while paling a little towards the edges. So delicate an appearance belies its toughness, for this is one of the most reliable of the shorter growing English Roses. It has a strong fragrance of myrrh and repeats very well. The breeding is Hybrid Tea 'Madame Caroline Testout' x (Floribunda 'Ma Perkins' x 'Constance Spry'). 'Madame Caroline Testout' was an early Hybrid Tea notable for its reliability, and something of this characteristic seems to have passed down to this variety. Austin (U.K.), 1969. See page 184.

WILLIAM SHAKESPEARE. This is a cross between 'The Squire' and 'Mary Rose'. At its best, it produces superb deep crimson blooms of neat full-petalled rosette formation. The growth is exceptionally strong and hardy but, like 'Fisherman's Friend', it has developed a tendency to blackspot, which is a great shame since it was a very hopeful line of development. Rich Old Rose fragrance. Height 4ft. Austin (U.K.), 1987.

* WINCHESTER CATHEDRAL. This is a sport from 'Mary Rose', to which it is similar in every way except that the flowers are white, with perhaps just the faintest tinge of buff at the centre later in the season. I think it is even more beautiful in white. See 'Mary Rose' above for further details. Named in aid of The Winchester Cathedral Trust. Austin (U.K.), 1988. See page 184.

WINDRUSH. Here we have a rose of quite a different character. A second generation descendant from 'Golden Wings', it is an English rose seeding x ('Canterbury' x 'Golden Wings'). The object of the cross was to produce a single flowered rose with some of the delicacy of a wild rose. It cannot quite be said that 'Windrush' is like a wild rose, but it does have large, almost single flowers of 5ins. across. They are pale lemon in colour with a handsome boss of light yellow stamens, and are produced with great freedom on a robust shrub. The foliage is plentiful

WIFE OF BATH, *a tough, short, reliable English Rose with medium-sized Old Rose blooms.*

WINCHESTER CATHEDRAL, *English Rose. A very desirable white sport from 'Mary Rose' and equally good in every way.*

WINDRUSH, *English Rose. Similar to 'Golden Wings' to which it is related, though stronger and more free flowering.*

YELLOW BUTTON, *English Rose. The flowers usually in deeper colours than seen here.*

THE REEVE, *an English Rose with cupped flowers and attractive arching growth.*

and pale green. The fragrance is similar to that of the Scottish Brier. Height 4ft. A first class shrub. Austin (U.K.), 1984. See page 185.

WISE PORTIA. A small bush with fairly large flowers of cupped formation. Their colour is a mixture of purple and mauve, sometimes of outstanding richness, at other times less so, varying according to the season, but always pleasing. The flowers are usually shapely and of true Old Rose character. Not particularly strong in growth, but it frequently produces blooms of exceptional beauty and has a delicious Old Rose fragrance. Height 2½ft. Bred from 'The Knight' x 'Glastonbury'. Austin (U.K.), 1982.

YELLOW BUTTON. A low growing shrub 2½ft. tall, with spreading, arching growth of at least as much across. The flowers are medium sized, of reflexing rosette formation, quartered, with a button-eye. The colour varies between light and deeper shades of yellow and there is often a distinct splash of yolk-yellow towards the centre. It has a strong, fruit-like fragrance. The foliage is pale green and glossy. Breeding 'Wife of Bath' x 'Chinatown'. Austin (U.K.), 1975. See page 185.

YELLOW CHARLES AUSTIN. This is, as the name suggests, a sport from 'Charles Austin' (see above). It is exactly the same, except that its flowers are pale yellow.

There are a number of other English Roses I do not include here, either because they have proved to be not up to standard, or because they have been superseded by a better variety. These include 'Admired Miranda', a very beautiful blush-pink variety with rather poor Hybrid Tea growth; 'Ellen', a quite good, large deep apricot-flowered rose; 'Glastonbury', a beautiful rich crimson rose at its best, but not sufficiently reliable; 'Immortal Juno', a large, globular-flowered rose of soft pink colouring which can be magnificent but easily becomes spoiled by the damp; 'Jaquenetta', a first class rose, but too much of a Floribunda, with apricot-blush, semi-double flowers in large bunches; 'Moonbeam', very similar to 'Jaquenetta', but with white flowers; 'The Friar', which has Hybrid Tea-like blooms opening to a rosette shape, but not sufficiently strong in growth; 'The Knight', deep crimson, subject to blackspot; 'The Miller', a reliable pink of inferior quality to more recent varieties; 'The Prioress', blush-pink; 'The Yeoman', perhaps the best of those listed here, which has flowers of a glistening soft pink and apricot colour, but is insufficiently reliable; and 'Troilus', with large flowers of honey-buff colouring — perhaps better for a warm climate.

Summer-flowering English Roses

In the course of breeding the English Roses it was inevitable that a number of good once-flowering varieties should occur. These are in the nature of a by-product, but I often wonder if it would not be worthwhile to breed them intentionally. I have spoken of the virtues of roses that only flower in midsummer in Chapter 2. We have introduced six such English Rose varieties at our nursery, each of which compares well with the Old Roses. I hope to do more in this direction in the future.

* CHIANTI. A tall, broad, well formed shrub of 6ft. in height and the same across, this rose is the result of a cross between the beautiful old crimson Gallica 'Tuscany', and the early Floribunda 'Dusky Maiden'. The flowers are large and of fully double rosette shape, their colour a dark crimson, becoming purplish-maroon as the flower ages, and there is a deep, rich Old Rose fragrance. It forms a robust, shapely shrub and flowers freely, and although it has to some extent been overshadowed by the better known 'Constance Spry', many people think it is rather better as a garden shrub. It was the basis from which most of the red English Roses were developed. Bred by Austin (U.K.), introduced jointly by Sunningdale Nurseries and David Austin Roses, 1967. See page 143.

* CONSTANCE SPRY. The result of a cross between the charming soft pink Gallica Rose 'Belle Isis' and the Floribunda 'Dainty Maid', this rose was an ancestor of the majority of the English Roses. It has truly magnificent flowers, in fact larger than any Old Rose I know, and yet they are never coarse or clumsy and are always in proportion to the shrub. Their colour is a lovely soft pink, and they are of full, deep Old Rose formation, the outer petals gradually reflexing. The growth is very strong, and it will, if left to its own devices, form a giant, sprawling shrub with large leaves and many thorns. It will require a good deal of space for development, growing to 7ft. in height, with an equal spread and, under good conditions, even more. It is, in fact, somewhat ungainly, and perhaps better grown as a Climber or over a fence; on a wall it will easily achieve 15ft. or more. However it is grown it will provide a magnificent sight, covering itself with giant blooms.

The flowers have a strong fragrance which has been described by Graham Thomas as being similar to that of myrrh, although some people have questioned this. Fragrance is hard to classify, but Graham Thomas did go to the trouble of obtaining myrrh in order to make the comparison, and he assures me his description is correct. Before the introduction of the English Roses, myrrh was a rare perfume among roses and its origin is interesting. I turn to the same source for my information: in Graham Thomas's opinion, the myrrh fragrance originates in the Ayrshire 'Splendens', and it would appear 'Belle Isis' must have had this latter rose somewhere in its ancestry. It may seem an odd combination but, from my experience in crossing very diverse roses, I would say it is entirely possible. Be all this as it may, the particular fragrance has persisted to a remarkable degree through the generations of 'Constance Spry's' progeny. Bred by Austin (U.K.), introduced jointly by Sunningdale Nurseries and Roses & Shrubs Limited of Albrighton, 1961.

DR. JACKSON. Earlier in this chapter I described the variety 'Red Coat'. 'Dr. Jackson' is a seedling from that rose and is in many ways an improvement on it, the flowers being of superior quality. These are single, of purest bright crimson and of a neatly rounded formation. The growth is more satisfactory than with 'Red Coat', being slightly arched and of more elegant appearance. It will produce a huge crop of blooms, in large, nicely formed sprays. I can think of few roses that would be more suitable for a position in the border where a distinct splash of crimson is required. It was named in memory of our much-loved local Doctor. Austin (U.K.), 1987.

DR. JACKSON, *English Rose.*
A good garden shrub
providing a splash of
dazzling colour.

CONSTANCE SPRY, *the first English Rose to be introduced, with large almost peony-sized blooms, on a large sprawling shrub. Also a good Climber. Summer flowering only.*

SHROPSHIRE LASS, *English Rose. A tall summer flowering shrub or climber.*

HILDA MURRELL. A strong, thorny shrub of 4 or 5ft. in height with large, rough-textured foliage. The flowers are large, with numerous petals, opening flat and of symmetrical formation. The colour is a remarkable deep glowing pink in the early stage, later becoming a little darker and losing some of its brightness. It is strikingly beautiful, of true Old Rose character and has a strong Old Rose fragrance. We named this rose after Miss Hilda Murrell not long before her tragic death in 1984. Miss Murrell was one of the pioneers of the reintroduction of the Old Roses after the Second World War. Austin (U.K.), 1984.

* LEANDER. A seedling from 'Charles Austin', which, in fact, looks very much like a smaller flowered version of that rose. The colour of the flowers is a very similar shade of deep apricot and there is the same strong fruit-like fragrance. The flowers are, however, of more perfect form, being a full rosette shape with their petals held in perfect spiral symmetry but, like 'Charles Austin', they lack something of the softness of character we look for in an Old Rose. They are held in large open sprays on a tall shrub of 8ft. or more in height. This is the most healthy and vigorous of all the English Roses, with shiny dark green disease-resistant foliage similar to that of a Modern Rose. As is so often the case with a large shrub of this kind, it flowers only occasionally after the first magnificent display. Austin (U.K.), 1982.

* SHROPSHIRE LASS. The result of a cross between the Hybrid Tea 'Madame Butterfly' and the Alba 'Madame Legras de St. Germain', this rose forms a tough shrub of some 8ft. in height, or it may be grown as a climber that will reach 15ft. on a wall. Its blush-white flowers are almost single, 4 or 5ins. across, with a large boss of stamens. Both leaves and growth show some sign of their Alba ancestry. This is a beautiful rose that deserves to be more widely grown, particularly as a climber, when its nicely poised flowers show off to maximum effect. Austin (U.K.), 1968. See page 189.

CHAPTER 6
English Roses
Now and in the Future

I n this Chapter I would like to go a little deeper into the nature of English Roses and to outline the ideal towards which they have been developed and, I hope, will be further developed in the future.

As I have already said, there is a large and growing band of gardeners who have a deep attachment to the Old Roses. It seems to me that it would be a shame if these roses, so different in their character to the roses of the present day, should remain, as it were, frozen in time. For one thing, there is no guarantee that they will retain their vigour over the years, although many of them have shown remarkable resilience up to the present time. More importantly, the Old Roses have a charm that has never been equalled by Modern Roses and this should continue to be developed.

It is this special beauty we find in Old Roses that I have tried to develop in the new English Roses. It might well be asked 'What is this beauty?' This is a difficult if not impossible question to answer – if you dissect them to find what makes them work, you tend to end with nothing more than a pile of spare parts. I will, however, try to make the attempt, if only because it is necessary that any type of rose should be based on certain principles if it is to have an identity.

May I first of all make it clear that it has not, and never has been, my intention to breed reproduction Old Roses. It would be quite possible to breed more Gallica Roses or Centifolia Roses and so on, and this would be a worthwhile undertaking if it is done with care and good taste, but this is not my objective. I do, however, wish them to have a character that is broadly in the mood of the Old Roses. They should have the softness, delicacy and charm of the Old Roses and, equally importantly, they should share their rich fragrance.

There is one point I should like to emphasise before going any further. I think that in the breeding of English Roses, or indeed any roses — or for that matter any other flower — we should approach this not just as a practical pursuit or as a science, but also as something in the nature of an art. 'Art' is a somewhat high-flown word, and ultimately perhaps

ENGLISH ROSES, *together with Polyantha types, are ideal for flower arrangements and, unlike most Old Roses, flower throughout the summer.*

a rather meaningless one, and I do not wish to sound pretentious; I only use it for the want of any better word. I think most people will see what I mean. In practice, the flower breeder does not have complete control of his craft; nature is not so accommodating. In spite of this, the breeder does have it in his power to push things in the general direction he may desire. He can at least select that which appeals to him— when he has the good fortune to find it, which is perhaps not much less than anyone can do in whatever their field of endeavour.

In the breeding of the English Roses it has always been my aim first of all to hybridize, and then to select for the overall beauty of the plant. That is to say, for the charm, character and fragrance of the flower; for the elegance and grace of growth and leaf. Only then do I consider the more practical aspects of reliability, toughness, disease resistance, and freedom and regularity of flowering, vital though these undoubtedly are. This, I believe, is the reverse of the practice of breeders in recent times. The tendency has too often been to see the rose as a machine for the production of flowers. The rose, it has been assumed, would automatically be beautiful. This unfortunately is not so. There has been a decline in the beauty of Modern Roses which has been reflected in a decline in the public's interest in them (although this decline has to some extent been offset by an increased interest in Shrub Roses). I really cannot see that the practical has much value without the aesthetic.

What then is the nature of an English Rose? What should be our aims and objectives for this group? The answer to these questions can be arranged under various headings: the form of the flower, their colour and their fragrance, the habit of growth, the foliage, and the way in which all these characteristics come together to form a whole, together with such practical considerations as recurrent flowering, vigour and freedom from disease, which make it all this possible.

Form of flower: In the English Roses we return to the open flower. It may or may not have attractive buds. If it does these will probably be round, opening to tight cups filled with developing petals. The buds can be charming, but it is in the open flower that the rose is most likely to reveal its full beauty. This is how it always was in the past — no different, in fact, to the form which we find in the peony or in many other flowers. One of the great advantages of such a flower formation is the long period over which it remains attractive, from the opening of the bud to the fall of the petals. Each day, indeed almost hourly, the flower is changing from one shape to another. Although this is also true of the early stages of the flowers of a Hybrid Tea, it ceases with the collapse of the bud. Not only does the English Rose hold its shape for a long period, there is also a greater variation between the varieties. Flowers may be deeply cupped or shallowly cupped; these cups may be filled with petals or they may be open, sometimes exposing their stamens to add further to the attraction. They may be rosette shaped — indeed the very word 'rosette' derives from the rose; such flowers may open flat, or the petals may recurve. Flowers may also be single or semi-double. Nor are we restricted to these forms; there are many gradations of shape between them. To me, such roses have an appeal that is not to be found in any other flower. Why this should be is hard to say, but it is probably due to the play of the light between the petals and, indeed, through the petals, which makes possible the most delightful and ever-changing effects.

Colour: The introduction of genes from *R. foetida* into the Hybrid

Teas led to a great deal of development in yellow shades. New and various colour combinations became possible, but unfortunately these did not always yield the best results. Mere multiplication of colours is not necessarily desirable in itself; the important thing is that the colours should be good colours, and colours suitable to roses. In the Modern Rose colours have too frequently tended to be harsh and metallic in appearance. With the English Roses we have returned to softer, and sometimes richer, shades which seem to us to be much more in keeping with the spirit of the rose. I am not against any particular colour, but just as we would take care in the choosing of colours for our homes, so we should be careful to choose suitable colours for our gardens and our roses. A colour that would be ideal for an iris would not necessarily be ideal for a rose. Moreover, many Modern Roses are in such harsh shades they do not mix well with other flowers. Worse than this, they do not mix well even with each other, and for this reason it is frequently recommended they should be planted in beds of one variety. This may be desirable at times, but it is sad that it should ever be a necessity, and in any case in most modern gardens it is not practical.

Fragrance: The fragrance of the English Roses is, I am pleased to say, particularly strong in the majority of varieties. This fortunately has not been too difficult to achieve. The Old Roses, from which in part English Roses spring, are, of course, noted for their fragrance, and this characteristic seems to persist down the generations, although I am always in fear of losing it. This can so easily happen — and has happened with other kinds of roses: a parent arises that is first class in every respect except fragrance, and because it is considered to be so good it is widely used for further breeding, thus reducing the fragrance of all its descendants.

The perfumes of roses are many — indeed it sometimes seems that all the fragrances of the garden are to be found in one or other rose species or variety, and many of them are to be found in the English Roses. The most unusual is that of 'Constance Spry' which, as I have said, is similar to that of myrrh, a scent that has proved very persistent in its descendants. From other sources comes the traditional Old Rose scent, the most rich and delicious of all fragrances; then there is the Tea Rose scent, the sharp scent of fresh fruit, the scent of the Scottish Brier and many shades between. I would like to think we might look forward to the time when we will breed for quality of scent as we now breed for quality of form. Scent is one of the most important aspects of a rose, but it is the one for which the breeder or nurseryman is least likely to be rewarded: it is difficult to describe, you cannot photograph it, and it is not very evident in the individual bloom at flower shows. People seldom buy a rose for its scent, although they will almost certainly be disappointed when they have it in their garden and find that it has none.

Growth and foliage: The Hybrid Teas brought with them an important innovation. Unlike all the roses that preceded them they were short bushes of some 3 to 3½ ft. in height that had to be hard pruned each year. Their chief purpose was as bedding plants — the rose bed became 'the thing'. No longer was the rose to be grown with other flowers, it was to have a place all to itself. Such growth and pruning does have one great advantage; it results in more continuous flowering. The disadvantage is that these bushes can never have the grace of their more shrubby forebears. The larger the plant, the greater its capacity for graceful growth. Taller, more bushy, more spreading or arching growth cannot but carry with it the possibility of a more elegant and graceful shrub. This is our aim with the English Roses. It has to be admitted that it is a difficult task to combine shrubbiness with recurrent flowering, at least in large shrubs, but a lot of progress has been made in this direction.

Foliage is no less important than growth. This may be not only beautiful in itself, but also provides the setting for the flower and has a vital effect on the appearance of the whole plant. It may differ between varieties in size, shape, colour and texture, and varying effects can be produced, thus adding greatly to the attractiveness and interest of the shrub. The English Roses, thanks to the diversity of their parentage, offer a wide range of foliage.

The reader may have noticed there is one theme running through the last few pages of this chapter, and that is variety. We should not be looking for a standardised rose, or for roses that conform to a standard set of requirements. Our aim should be to create as much variation as possible between different roses. For the breeder, of course, it is often necessary to work on one theme for many generations, but within roses as a whole I should like to see developments in many different directions, whether it be in flower, growth or leaf. Variety, we are told, is the spice of life and with roses this is particularly true. They are now planted so widely and are to be found in so many gardens, that if we do not have this variety there is a grave danger people will become bored through sheer repetition and over-familiarity. This has to be guarded against, and more especially in our time when it is convenient and more profitable for commercial growers to mass produce a small number of varieties and foist them on the public — whether they like them or not. *Practical considerations:* Finally, we must consider what I have called the practical aspects of roses: their ability to grow, flower and resist disease. A rose that will not grow properly is of very little use to anyone, and it has to be admitted that some of the earlier English Roses were lacking in this respect. There were good genetic reasons for this. It is not possible to start at the beginning again, as it were, and have all the virtues at once. However, in breeding English Roses, we do have one advantage in that we do not have to strive for a bud flower form, as is the case with the Hybrid Teas, and this does relieve us of a very considerable restriction. The drive for a particular form of flower makes it more difficult for us to develop other important qualities. With the English Roses a wide variety of species and classes of roses can be involved in their make up, without necessarily losing the desired shape of flower. The use of a wide range of roses has opened up greater possibilities. It has also afforded a degree of hybrid vigour. These factors help to make strong and healthy English Roses possible.

Disease resistance in English Roses is comparable to that of the Floribundas. It is an unfortunate but inescapable fact that repeat-flowering roses are more liable to disease than non-repeating. The main diseases of the rose are mildew and blackspot, both of which develop easily on young growth. The repeat-flowering rose is, by its very nature, always producing new growth in order to make more flowers. Thus we have a continual supply of soft young growth, making it easy for a disease to move from an older leaf to a new leaf as the season progresses, multiplying as it goes. With a non-recurrent rose it is quite different. These produce growth and retire for the year, leaving the leaves hard and disease resistant. With a repeat flowering Shrub Rose the problem is even greater than with Hybrid Teas. A Bush Rose is pruned very low, leaving little old growth to carry disease on into the following season. With a Shrub Rose, if it is to remain a shrub, we have to leave more growth, and thus there is a greater chance of the disease continuing. Having said this, I would not like the reader to think disease in repeat-flowering Shrub Roses is necessarily a great problem.

It is sometimes said that, other than in minor areas, there is not much scope left in roses for further development. Nothing could be further from the truth. The rose is a genus of such wealth and variety that the possibilities are almost endless. The English Roses are an example and it would be nice to think that other breeders might take them up, for only then can they come to their full potential. There is ample room for development. Should breeders do this, my only concern is that they should devote themselves to the aesthetic qualities I have been describing, as well as to the practical. There can be little doubt that if they were to treat English Roses as so many flowers have been treated in recent times, their last state might well be worse than our first. It is not difficult to visualise giant gaudily-coloured, open roses, like huge dahlias on short bushes. Such horrors are well within the capacity of the rose and might even, for a short time, gain popularity.

It is sad to say that a great deal of what the plant breeder touches turns to dross. How many flowers have been taken up by the plant breeder and gained a short popularity, only to sink back into obscurity? Giant over-sized dahlias and chrysanthemums, lolloping gladioli, huge, frilly, collapsing irises, blinding geraniums and so on. Consider, too, the humble polyanthus, with its once simple charm bred from the cowslip and the primrose. How are these now? The truth is that flower breeders tend to be concerned with the more and more, while they should be concerned with the better and more beautiful. There must be a point where the search for more flowers, larger flowers, or brighter flowers becomes counter-productive and eventually ends in the downfall of the flower concerned. In time, the public always tire of such productions and true values reassert themselves. We should try to discern the essential spirit of a flower and develop it. This, of course, is no easy matter, but it provides a field that is almost endless in its extent.

CHAPTER 7
Rose Cultivation

Growing Old or English Roses is not difficult. It is easy to surround it with a mystery that is not warranted. Good results can be achieved with little more than common sense and a minimum of attention. In fact, many who grow roses do so with no more than this. In spite of this a little extra skill, care and knowledge will help us to achieve better results. One thing is certain, the more we put into our roses, the more pleasure we shall get out of them.

Choice of Site

The choice of position for roses depends in part on aesthetic, and in part on practical considerations. There are certain conditions that roses do not like. They do not like shade, not even partial shade, although, as we have already seen, there are some roses that will withstand this better than others. They do not like competition from tree roots, nor do they like the drip from the outer edges of trees. Both English and Old Roses look particularly well when mixed with other plants and shrubs, but it is very necessary to take care that these others are not such as might compete too strongly with the roses. This is particularly important when the roses are first planted; once they have risen above their neighbours it is rather less crucial. The soil should be of reasonable depth and in good condition. It should also be well drained. It is not possible to grow roses in waterlogged soil. The Roses in Chapter 2, that is to say the non-repeat flowering Old Roses, will usually withstand poorer conditions than the repeat-flowering Old Roses (Chapter 3) and the English Roses (Chapter 5). This is because the repeat-flowering roses have a much more strenuous task in providing continuous flushes of bloom.

Soil Preparation

Usually the gardener does not have much choice as regards soil type. He has to make the best of what is there. Without doubt most roses are happiest in a heavier soil where they will grow far larger and more strongly than in other soils. With adequate manuring, good results should be easily obtained. If you have an exceptionally heavy clay this may cause some difficulty at first, but it can be overcome by mixing in liberal quantities of humus and by using a planting mixture around the roots of the rose.

Light soils and medium loams are entirely suitable, but the roses will require more generous treatment, particularly if the soil is very light.

The real problems arise in limy or chalky soils. Roses do not like too much lime. They prefer a soil that is either neutral or very slightly acid. As a nurseryman, I am sometimes a little dismayed when I meet our customers — so many of them seem to have chalk gardens, and I cannot help wondering how our roses are faring. Fortunately this is a problem that can be overcome, but it does require some expenditure and effort. Large quantities of humus should be mixed with the soil, particularly immediately around the rose, although it is better if this does not actually touch the roots. The humus will neutralize the alkalinity and help retain moisture.

Peaty soils are the most difficult of all. Here, the only solution is to import soil and place it in the area around the rose to a depth of 1ft.

Care in the preparation of the soil is very worthwhile. In planting roses, we are making a long term investment, and it will really pay dividends if we do the job thoroughly. If the soil can be dug some weeks before the roses arrive, so much the better. Thorough cultivation to a spade's depth, together with the careful mixing of soil and humus, will make a great difference. In addition to this, it is worth breaking up the subsoil with a fork as you dig; this will help drainage and enable the deep tap roots to go well down. If you dig up an old rose bush you will usually find that there are few roots in the first foot of soil; most of the growth is deep down. In spite of this, the humus should only be mixed with the top 12ins. of soil; beneath this it will be unable to work effectively.

The reader will have noticed the emphasis I place on humus. I regard this as crucial in growing good roses. Its use is not really necessary with very strong roses such as the Species, but with repeat-flowering roses like English Roses or Bourbon Roses, and to a lesser extent Old Roses, it is essential if we are to get the best results, particularly later in the year. The humus may take various forms: well-rotted farmyard manure, compost, one of the various proprietary brands, or peat. The first two are best, but peat is a good alternative. It is not a bad plan to use peat together with the other forms of humus. It is very long lasting and has a good effect on the condition of the soil, mixing in well, but has little nutritional value.

If you are unable to apply humus, at least use a proprietary rose fertilizer. Indeed, a dressing of fertilizer early in the spring after planting will be desirable in any case. Potash is vital for roses, particularly on light soils which tend to be deficient in this. Heavy soils often lack phosphates. Sulphate of potash is a good source of potash, and bone meal an excellent natural source of phosphates.

Replanting Roses in the Same Ground

There is one point above all I would like every rose grower to heed. When the soil has had roses grown in it for any length of time, say five or six years or more, it should not be replanted with roses. Such soils will be what is usually known as 'rose sick'. This does not mean the existing roses will not thrive in it indefinitely, but when the ground is replanted with new roses, it is quite probable that they will fail to grow properly. This is true even when extremely healthy and robust roses have been taken out. The exact nature of the problem is not fully understood; it is almost certainly due to microscopic organisms known as nematodes, but poisons from the roots of the previous roses may also be involved.

Fortunately this only concerns the area immediately around the bush or shrub. If it is possible to move even a little way to one side of the previous rose, there should be no problem. Where this is not practical the answer is to remove the soil from the area where the original rose has been, to a width of about 2 to 4ft. across, and 1ft. in depth, according to the size of the rose, and replace this with a mixture of one part humus to three parts good soil from another area of the garden. Where rose beds are involved, it will be necessary to remove all the soil and replace it. This may seem a little extreme, but I think it is worthwhile. Far better, if you can, to move your new roses to a different part of the garden. Another more simple method is to sterilize the soil before planting. It is possible to obtain chemicals especially for this purpose from your garden centre.

For those who do not feel inclined to go to these lengths, the problem can be mitigated by the use of large quantities of humus. The problem of rose sickness is greater in light soils that tend to lack humus and, in my experience, much less in humus-rich soils.

Purchasing Roses

There are two ways in which roses can be purchased — bare rooted or in containers. There is now a generation of gardeners which tends to know only the latter, or to think there is something rather risky about the former. This is quite wrong; both have their virtues, but on balance I would favour the bare rooted. Roses are never really happy in containers, and unless the garden centre has looked after them well, there is a danger they may be poor specimens.

If you require roses that are in any way out of the ordinary, it will be necessary to buy through mail order — unless you are lucky enough to live near to a suitable rose specialist. It is not practical for the average garden centre to carry any more than a very limited range. When buying from a rose specialist it is advisable to order well in advance. The grower has to plan his crop some two and a half years ahead, and it is not always possible to predict what the demand will be. Varieties will inevitably become sold out.

Planting

I will deal with the bare-rooted roses first. These may be planted at any time between November and March. If they are not purchased locally, they may arrive either at a time when you are not able to plant them immediately, or when the weather or soil conditions are not suitable. In this case, they should be temporarily heeled into the ground by digging a small trench and covering the roots with soil. They will then be quite safe for many weeks. If the soil is frozen when the roses arrive, they will be all right in their packet for three or four weeks, so long as they are kept in a cool but frost-proof building.

Planting should be at such a depth that the joint at which the rose has been budded on to the root stock is just beneath the surface of the soil.

Make a hole of adequate size to take the roots, spread the roots out evenly, and fill in with soil, treading it down gently with the feet, being careful not to get the soil too solid. It is very worthwhile using a special planting mixture for this purpose. This can be made up of half peat and half best garden soil, together with a sprinkling of bone meal. Alternatively, a ready-made mixture may be bought. This will give your rose a much better start and, incidentally, if your mixture is kept dry, make it possible for you to plant when the soil and weather conditions are less than perfect.

If you wish to move established plants, this is entirely possible providing they are not too old and gnarled. Roses often seem to relish this treatment. Before doing this, it is vital to prune the bush very severely, removing all old and dead wood, and cutting it almost to the ground. This will mean that the roots of the plant, which will have inevitably been badly maimed, will not have to maintain too much growth in the early stages.

The planting of container-grown bushes is very much the same as for those with bare roots, except that it is important to avoid breaking up the soil when removing the bush from the pot. It is best to cut away the plastic with a knife, or, if the container is a solid pot, to knock the bush and soil out whole. The advantage of a container rose is that it can be planted at any time of the year. Having said that, it has to be pointed out that such roses, when planted later than June, will by the following year usually be little further ahead than a bare-rooted rose that has been planted the following winter.

If we are planting late in the season, say late March or early April, it is advisable to keep an eye on soil moisture. The ground can easily become dry before the roses have had time to make roots. In such cases give a heavy watering that will go deep. This is doubly important in the case of container roses that are planted out of season. It is easy to think that they are quite safe in their little ball of soil, but this can quickly dry out.

Pruning

My remarks in the first paragraph of this chapter are particularly pertinent here. Pruning is not difficult, and much latitude is possible. It is something of an art and it can be interpreted, in some degree at least, according to the type of growth that is required. Used in this way, it becomes an interesting and enjoyable task. I have from time to time, while progressing through the various classes of roses, made notes on the subject, but it would perhaps be convenient to summarise it here in a more general way.

OLD ROSES THAT DO NOT REPEAT FLOWER (Chapter 2). It is possible to leave these virtually unpruned, although a fairly substantial thinning of older, less-productive wood will become necessary after a few years. This will make way for new and more vigorous growth. At the same time it may be desirable to shape the shrub according to your own taste. Different people may interpret this in different ways. It may be thought worthwhile to preserve elegantly protruding branches, even if this upsets the symmetry of the whole. If pruned in this way Old Roses may become too large for many gardens, and although they will provide a mass of bloom, they will not produce the finest or largest individual flowers should such be required. A more usual method is to cut back the strong main growth by about one-third of its length, at the same time cutting the side shoots to one-third and removing the old, dead and spent wood completely. In this way you will obtain a more compact, although sometimes less elegant, shrub.

All these roses are best pruned as soon after flowering as possible. This encourages new growth, which will in turn produce the best flowers in the following season.

REPEAT-FLOWERING SHRUB ROSES. In so far as their pruning require-ments are concerned, repeat-flowering Shrub Roses (by which I mean the English Roses and the roses in Chapter 3 — Chinas, Portlands, Bourbons and Hybrid Perpetuals) usually present quite a different problem to pruning Old Roses that do not repeat flower. Their long season of bloom makes heavier demands upon them, and closer attention is desirable. It is necessary to remove the small, twiggy side shoots and, at the same time, to cut away some of the old growth to encourage the new. Be careful not to remove too many or too much of the stronger branches in the early stages (as these will form the structure of the shrub) or the rose may fail to become a shrub at all. Something of what I have said about the roses that do not repeat flower applies to those that do repeat flower. Try to avoid a too-clipped appearance — there is no virtue in pruning for pruning's sake. We are trying to produce an attractive, shapely shrub.

China Roses require little pruning, other than the removal of some of the old wood. Hybrid Perpetuals often make tall, upright bushes, and with such roses growth may have to be reduced to half its length in order to achieve a presentable shrub. English Roses include a whole variety of different habits of growth, and pruning is dealt with at some length in the introduction to Chapter 5, but broadly speaking it is the same as for other repeat-flowering Shrub Roses.

Pruning should be done during the winter, to enable the shrub to make an early start and have time to produce two or three crops of flowers.

Mulching, Feeding and Watering

This is not entirely essential for once-flowering Old Roses, although these will be greatly improved by such attention. With repeat-flowering Old Roses and English Roses it becomes very necessary if we are to have quality and continuity of flowering. It is true that acceptable results can be achieved without such care, but a little extra assistance in this direction yields results out of all proportion to the effort involved. This is particularly true with soils that are less favourable to roses: light sands, chalk, limestone, and so on.

Mulching is the most important. If roses are given a good mulch each year, or even every other year, most other cultural considerations fade into insignificance. Mulching helps to maintain the moisture in the soil through drier periods, and this makes continual flowering possible. It provides plant food, it reduces susceptibility to black spot, and has a smothering effect on weeds. Various materials can be used. Rotted compost is excellent. It is worthwhile gathering your garden and household waste for this purpose, but it should be given ample time to rot down. Perhaps the simplest method is to use bought materials such as peat or forest bark. These are free from weeds and easy to handle. The feeding value will be less, but this can be corrected by the application of fertilizers.

When growth begins in the spring, a dressing of one or other of the various proprietary rose fertilizers should be applied. This should be repeated in June or July as the first flush of flowers is passing in order to encourage the next. A good general fertilizer is suitable, but it should contain a high proportion of potash, particularly on light land. Roses demand large quantities of potash, more than most other plants.

Many people who grow repeat-flowering Old Roses and English Roses are disappointed to find that their plants frequently fail to make a second crop. Obviously we cannot have repeat flowering without growth, and growth is entirely dependent on the availability of moisture. It is of little use applying fertilizer to a rose if there is not the moisture to make it available to the plant. Even in a climate like our own, there is rarely sufficient rain to maintain moisture at the necessary levels throughout the summer. I am certainly not going to suggest that watering is anything like essential in Britain, but it can contribute considerably to the performance of our roses. In drier climates it is of course vital. There are excellent automatic watering systems available which will make the task very simple, and they are not expensive. If you do decide to water, give a good soaking. In this country, even one or two such soakings in the course of an average summer will make all the difference. This is particularly important after the first flush of flowers.

Suckers and Dead Heading

Most roses are budded on to root stocks and this inevitably means that from time to time there will be suckers, that is to say growth from the stock. Suckers are not difficult to detect, as their leaves are usually very different from those of the garden variety. With the Alba Roses we can more easily be deceived, as they are closely related to *Rosa canina* from which most of the root stocks we use in this country have been developed. In other countries *R. multiflora* and other stocks are used, and these are easily detected. A great deal of trouble will be saved if suckers are removed early on; it is much easier at this stage, and little of the energy of the plant will have been wasted. A knife is the best tool for this purpose — try to cut away a little of the bark together with the sucker, otherwise the sucker will quickly re-emerge from the same point.

The removal of dead flowers is not essential, but the plant retains a much tidier appearance if this is done. Roses are by nature single flowered, but man has made them into double flowered. For this reason the petals tend to stay intact even as the flower dies, and they are often unsightly.

Dead heading is more important in the case of repeat-flowering shrubs such as the English Roses and the old repeat-flowering groups, for if these produce hips they will take up the energy of the plant and inhibit further flowering.

Diseases and Pests

Considering how widely the rose is grown it cannot be said that it is particularly subject to diseases and pests. By and large, the rose is able to live with most of them. They become more of a problem when many roses are grown in close proximity. This is, of course, true of nearly all plants. We hear a great deal about elaborate spraying, but this is not always essential, although it is more important with the repeat-flowering roses.

Perhaps the biggest problem is blackspot. Few roses are completely resistant to this disease, and it might be said to be the greatest single drawback of the rose. Anyone who can breed roses that will resist blackspot will be doing a great service. Unfortunately in the breeding of such resistance we can lose many other desirable characteristics.

With modern sprays and equipment, control both of diseases and pests is not too much of a hardship. The important point is to start spraying early in the season. Most problems start in quite a small way but quickly mutliply. If you can halt them at an early stage, treatment will be much easier and more effective.

DISEASES

BLACKSPOT (*Diplocarpon rosae*). The symptoms of this disease are just as the name suggests — black patches appear on the leaves, with yellow at the edges. These will grow and multiply and may, if left unattended, defoliate the whole plant. Blackspot is worse in the country or in any area where the air is clean, but some varieties are much more susceptible than others.

The most effective spray at present is one which contains bupirimate-triforine. This should be applied as directed both on leaves and stems, at the time when the leaves are emerging. This early spraying is most important. It is then recommended that spraying should continue at ten to fourteen day intervals, but this is a counsel of perfection. With most roses, a further two sprayings at the normal rate in late May, June and July will keep the disease sufficiently in check.

Good cultivation will help in the avoidance of blackspot. Adequate feeding and mulching is important, but avoid the excessive use of nitrogen. Poor drainage and the shade of trees will also encourage this disease.

POWDERY MILDEW (*Sphaerotheca pannosa*). A white powdery mould appears on the leaves and buds. The leaves may turn yellow and purple and eventually wither and drop prematurely. The buds may fail to open. Use a spray containing bupirimate-triforine as soon as the disease appears, and continue as suggested for blackspot. Do not allow mildew to develop too much before spraying.

Here again, good cultivation encourages healthy growth. Mulching, watering and feeding will help to prevent the problem in the first place. Excessive nitrogen provides soft growth which mildew thrives upon.

ROSE RUST (*Phragmidium tuberculatum* and other species). This is one of the worst diseases, but fortunately is not common. Orange swellings appear both on upper and lower leaf surfaces in spring. Later in the season, rust-like patches appear on the underside of the leaf and eventually turn black in August.

Normally you will not have to worry about this problem, but where it does occur it is important to catch it early. Spray in mid- to early May, when the first infection appears. An effective spray is one which contains oxycarboxin. It is vital to spray the underside of the leaf — the upperside is not important.

Rose rust occurs most frequently on hot, dry soils and where the soil is deficient in potash. It occurs more often in a wet season, or where there is a prolonged heavy dew. Certain varieties of rose are much more subject to it than others. Alba Roses and Rugosa Roses, which are normally so trouble-free, may be affected.

PESTS

APHIDS. These may be green, orange, reddish or black. Most gardeners will be familiar with them. They feed off young shoots, starting in the spring, and multiply rapidly if not checked. Eventually they will cause distortion of the leaf. Excreted honeydew dropped on the leaves often grows a black fungus known as 'Sooty Mould'.

Control is not difficult, and numerous systemic sprays are available. Spray when the insects first appear. When purchasing, make sure that the chemical is not a hazard to bees or other useful insects.

LEAF-ROLLING SAWFLY. The leaflets become tightly rolled and a greyish-green grub may be found inside. This problem chiefly occurs where roses are in the shade of trees.

It is only possible to spray for prevention before the curling of the leaf occurs. When you have this problem it will be necessary to wait until the following year and spray in May with a spray containing fenitrothion.

Having provided this short list of troubles, it is important to stress that we should not regard rose growing as a continual battle with diseases and insects. Often these will not occur. We only need to treat them where they show signs of becoming a real problem.

Glossary

ANTHER. The part of the flower which produces pollen; the upper section of the stamen.

ARCHING SHRUB. A shrub in which the long main branches bend down towards the soil, usually in a graceful manner.

BALLED, BALLING. The clinging together of petals due to damp, so that the bloom fails to open.

BARE-ROOT ROSES. Roses bought without soil, not in a container.

BASAL SHOOT. The strong main shoot that arises from the base of the rose.

BICOLOUR. A rose bloom with two distinct shades of colour.

BOSS. The bunch of stamens at the centre of a flower.

BRACT. A modified leaf at the base of a flower stalk.

BREAK. New growth from a branch.

BUDDING. The usual method for the propagation of roses by the grafting of a leaf bud on to the neck of a root stock.

BUD UNION. The point on the root stock where the bud of the garden rose was inserted.

BUSHY SHRUB. A rose of dense, rounded growth.

BUTTON EYE. A button-like fold of petals in the centre of a rose.

CALYX. The green protective cover over the flower bud which opens into five sepals.

CHROMOSOMES. Chains of linked genes contained in the cells of plants and animals.

CROSS. See Hybrid.

DIE BACK. The progressive dying back of a shoot from the tip.

DIPLOID. A plant with two sets of chromosomes.

FLORE PLENO. Double flower.

FLUSH. A period of blooming.

GENE. A unit of heredity controlling inherited characteristics of a plant.

GENUS. A group of plants having common characteristics, e.g. *Rosa*.

HEELING IN. Temporary planting of roses when conditions are not suitable for permanent planting.

HEIGHT. The heights given for individual varieties are only approximate. Much will depend on soil, site, season and geographic area. The breadth of a rose bush or shrub will usually be slightly less than the height.

HIPS OR HEPS. Seed pods of a rose.

HYBRID. A rose resulting from crossing two different species or varieties.

LEAFLETS. The individual section of a leaf.

MODERN APPEARANCE, ROSE OF. Rose that usually has high-pointed buds and smooth foliage, similar to a Hybrid Tea Rose.

MUTATION. See Sport.

OLD APPEARANCE, ROSE OF. Rose with bloom of cupped or rosette shape, rather than the pointed bud and informal flower of a Modern Rose; the plant usually having rough textured leaves, i.e. Gallica, Centifolia, etc.

ORGANIC FERTILIZER. A fertilizer made from natural materials rather than chemicals.

PERPETUAL FLOWERING. A rose that continues to flower in the same year after the first flush of bloom, though not necessarily continually.

PISTIL. Female organ of a flower consisting of the stigma, style and ovary.

POLLEN PARENT. The male parent of a variety.

POMPON. A small rounded bloom with regular short petals.

QUARTERED. A flower in which the centre petals are folded into four quarters.

QUILLED PETALS. Petals folded in the form of a quill.

RECESSIVE GENE. A gene that is dominated by another, rendering it ineffective.

RECURRENT FLOWERING. See Perpetual Flowering.

REMONTANT. See Perpetual Flowering.

REPEAT FLOWERING. See Perpetual Flowering.

ROOTS, ROSES ON THEIR OWN. Not budded on to a stock; grown from cuttings.

ROOT STOCK (STOCK). The host plant on to which a cultivated variety is budded.

SCION. A shoot or bud used for grafting on to a root stock.

SEEDLING. A rose grown from seed. In the context of this book, the offspring of a variety.

SEPAL. One of the five green divisions of the calyx.

SHRUB. A rose that is normally pruned lightly and allowed to grow in a more natural form, as opposed to a bush which is pruned close to the ground.

SPORT. A change in the genetic make up of the plant, as for example when a pink rose suddenly produces a white flower.

SPREADING SHRUB. A shrub on which the branches tend to extend outwards rather than vertically.

STAMEN. The male organ of a flower, consisting of the filament and anther, which produces pollen.

STIGMA. The end of the pistil or female flower organ.

STYLE. The stem of the pistil which joins the stigma to the ovary.

SUCKER. A shoot growing from the root stock instead of from the budded variety.

TETRAPLOID. A plant with four sets of chromosomes.

TRIPLOID. A plant with three sets of chromosomes.

UPRIGHT SHRUB. A rose in which the growth tends to be vertical.

VARIETY. Strictly speaking, a naturally occurring variation of a species. The popular meaning, so far as roses are concerned, is a distinct type of rose.

Main Agents for English Roses

The following nurseries are main agents, in their respective countries, for English Roses. English Roses are also available from numerous other nurseries and garden centres in these and other countries.

UNITED KINGDOM
* David Austin Roses,
  Bowling Green Lane,
  Albrighton,
  Wolverhampton WV7 3HB,
  England.

FRANCE
Georges Delbard,
Malicorne,
03600 Commentry,
Paris, France.

GERMANY
* Ingwer J. Jensen,
  Hermann-Lons-Weg 39,
  D-2390 Flensburg,
  West Germany.

ITALY
Rose Barni,
51100 Pistoia,
Via Autostrada 5,
Italy.

HOLLAND
Kwekerij 't Hulder (trade only),
5821 EE Vierlingsbeek,
Overloonseweg lla,
Holland.

De Wilde Bussum (retail only),
Kwekerij Pr.,
Irenelaan 14,
P.O. Box 115,
1400 A.C. Bussum,
Holland.

SWITZERLAND
* Richard Huber AG,
  Baumschulen,
  5605 Dottikon,
  Postcheck 50-11595-1,
  Switzerland.

AUSTRALIA
The Perfumed Garden Pty. Ltd.,
47 Rendelsham Avenue,
Mt. Eliza, 3930,
Australia.

CANADA
* Hortico Inc.,
Robson Road,
R.R.I. Waterdown,
LOR 2HO,
Canada.

NEW ZEALAND
* Trevor Griffiths & Sons Ltd.,
No. 3 R.D.,
Timaru,
New Zealand.

SOUTH AFRICA
* Ludwigs Roses C.C.,
P.O. Box 28165,
Sunnyside,
Pretoria 0132,
South Africa.

U.S.A.
* Wayside Gardens,
Hodges,
South Carolina 29695-0001,
U.S.A.

Nurseries marked * also grow a wide selection of Old and Shrub Roses.

Appellations for English Roses

To meet legal requirements, roses that have been patented have been allocated an alternative name, so that if a roses's name has been changed either in the U.K. or any other part of the world, it will still be identifiable.

Abraham Darby (Auscot)
Ambridge Roses (Auswonder)
Bibi Maizoon (Ausdimindo)
Bow Bells (Ausbells)
Brother Cadfael (Ausglobe)
Cardinal Hume (Harregale)
Charles Rennie Mackintosh (Ausren)
Claire Rose (Auslight)
Cottage Rose (Ausglisten)
Country Living (Auscountry)
Emily (Ausburton)
English Garden (Ausbuff)
Evelyn (Aussaucer)
Financial Times Centenary (Ausfin)
Fisherman's Friend (Auschild)
Gertrude Jekyll (Ausbord)
Glamis Castle (Auslevel)
Golden Celebration (Ausgold)
Graham Thomas (Ausmas)
Heritage (Ausblush)
Jayne Austin (Ausbreak)
Kathryn Morley (Ausvariety)
L.D. Braithwaite (Auscrim)
Lilac Rose (Auslilac)
Mary Rose (Ausmary)
Othello (Auslo)
Peach Blossom (Ausblossom)

Queen Nefertiti (Ausap)
Redouté (Auspale)
St. Cecilia (Ausmit)
Sharifa Asma (Ausreef)
Sir Edward Elgar (Ausprima)
Sir Walter Raleigh (Ausspry)
Swan (Auswhite)
Sweet Juliet (Ausleap)
The Countryman (Ausman)
The Dark Lady (Ausbloom)
The Herbalist (Aussemi)
The Pilgrim (Auswalker)
The Prince (Ausvelvet)
Warwick Castle (Auslian)
Winchester Cathedral (Auscat)

Bibliography

American Rose Society's *Annuals,* from 1917.

Bean, W.J., *Trees and Shrubs Hardy in the British Isles,* 8th edn. revised.

Bunyard, A.E., *Old Garden Roses,* Collingridge, 1936.

Dobson, B.R., *Combined Rose List. Hard to Find Roses and Where to Find Them,* Beverly R. Dobson, Irvington, New York 10533, 1985.

Edwards, G., *Wild and Old Garden Roses,* David & Charles, Newton Abbot, 1975; Hafner, New York, 1975.

Fletcher, H.L.V., *The Rose Anthology,* Newnes, 1963.

Foster-Melliar, Rev. A., *The Book of the Rose,* Macmillan, 1894; 1910.

Gault S.M. and Synge P.M., *The Dictionary of Roses in Colour,* Michael Joseph and Ebury Press, 1970.

Gore, C.F., *The Book of Roses or The Rose Fancier's Manual,* 1838; Heyden, 1978.

Griffiths, Trevor, *The Book of Old Roses,* Michael Joseph, 1984.

Griffiths, Trevor, *The Book of Classic Old Roses,* Michael Joseph, 1986.

Harkness, Jack, *Roses,* Dent, 1978.

Hillier's *Manual of Trees and Shrubs,* 4th edn., 1974.

Hole, S. Reynolds, *A Book about Roses,* William Blackwood, 1896.

Jekyll, G. and Mawley, E., *Roses for English Gardens,* Country Life, 1902; reprinted Woodbridge 1982.

Keays, F.L., *Old Roses,* Macmillan, New York, 1935; facsimile edn. Heyden, Philadelphia and London, 1978.

Krussman, G., *Roses,* English edn., Batsford, 1982.

McFarland, J.H., *Modern Roses,* 8th edn., McFarland Co., U.S.A., 1980.

McFarland, J.H., *Roses of the World in Colour,* Cassell, 1936.

Mansfield, T.C., *Roses in Colour and Cultivation,* Collins, 1947.

Nottle, T., *Growing Old Fashioned Roses in Australia and New Zealand,* Kangaroo Press, 1983.

Paul, William, *The Rose Garden,* 10th edn., Simpkin, Marshall, Hamilton, Kent & Co., 1903.

Pemberton, Rev. J.H., *Roses, Their History, Development and Cultivation,* Longmans Green 1908; rev. edn. 1920.

Redouté, P.J., *Les Roses,* 1817-24.

Ridge, A., *For the Love of a Rose,* Faber & Faber, 1965.

Rivers, T., *The Rose Amateur's Guide,* Longmans Green, 1837.

Rose Growers' Association, *Find that Rose.*

Ross, D., *Shrub Roses in Australia,* Deane Ross, 1981.

Royal National Rose Society's *Annuals,* from 1911.

Shepherd, R., *History of the Rose,* Macmillan, New York, 1966.

Steen, N., *The Charm of Old Roses,* Herbert Jenkins, 1966.

Thomas, G.S., *The Old Shrub Roses,* Phoenix House, 1955.

Thomas, G.S., *Shrub Roses of Today,* Phoenix House, 1962.

Thomas, G.S., *Climbing Roses Old and New,* Phoenix House, 1965.

Thompson, Richard, *Old Roses for Modern Gardens,* Van Nostrand, New York, 1959.

Index

(figures in italics indicate an illustration)